MW01136215

MAUI WRITERS INK

Short Stories & Poems

© 2019 Maui Writers Ink Publishing
Lahaina, Hawaii

Maui Writers Ink / Short Stories & Poems

Copyright © 2019 by Maui Writers Ink
All rights reserved.
Except for use in any review,
the reproduction of this book in printed,
electronic or film is a violation of copyright law.

Second Edition
ISBN - 9781093985375

Publishing Editors
William Sayles captsails@aol.com
Lisa Downey lisadowneywrites@gmail.com

Illustrations by Nansy Phleger

Cover painting by Lowell Mapes, Private Collection

Layout design by Lisa Downey

T. A. Binkley

[signature]

Enjoy the read

Jo Ann Carroll

Lynette Chun

.

Lisa Downey

Elaine Gallant

Oliver Gold

John Noah Hoʻomanawanui

Nansy Phleger

To Wendy from one author, to another!

Remote islands isolated by vast seas have long attracted the seafarer, the dreamer, the artist, and the teller of tall tales along with the colorful folk of dubious past deeds, some of whom gather fortnightly to share their thoughts and creativity as the Maui Writers Ink. We hope you enjoy our stories. Some will make you laugh, some might make you cry, and some could make you think and reflect upon how—and why—you came to Maui, too.

—Nansy Phleger

With aloha

Nancy Phleger

Contents

Oliver Gold

T. A. Binkley

Nansy Phleger

*   2016 Lahainatown Action Committee Short Story Competition, 1st place.
**   2015 Lahainatown Action Committee Short Story Competition, 2nd place.
*** 2014 Lahainatown Action Committee Short Story Competition, 2nd place.

On the Corner of
Front Street and Paradise

Lisa Downey

You need to be living in Hawaii.

You know the expression "it hit me out of the blue"? Nothing in my experience had ever come close to literally doing that…until that day. It wasn't a thought. It was as if a neurosurgeon had injected it into the core of my gray matter:

You need to be living in Hawaii.

Divine inspiration? Spirit guiding me? I decided it would not be wise, and actually quite arrogant, to ignore the message.

I told my husband, Len, and he responded with something like "Okay. Let's go." He'd vacationed in Hawaii for a number of years, escaping the frigid Canadian winter for two weeks of thawing-out on Maui. He didn't need convincing.

I had only ever been to Molokai (that's a different story) via Honolulu airport.

Two years after that initial thought of moving to Hawaii prompted me, we finally sold our house (which we had planned to do anyway), left our sweet kitty with family, then flew to Maui for a "trial residence." We rented a room from Lori, a single mom and her seven-year-old daughter, Noelle.

I told Lori how the "command suggestion" to move to Hawaii had struck me two years earlier. "That's Maui magic at work," she said.

I hadn't heard of Maui magic, but if that's what drove me here I was ready for more magic!

Just two weeks into our two-month experiment, we decided we definitely wanted to live in Maui and spent the rest of our stay scouting the area for places to live and investigating job prospects. We signed a rental agreement for an apartment in Kihei before we returned to South Carolina to pack our belongings into a forty-foot container.

We were committed.

There was next to nothing work-wise on Maui, but we were determined to "make it happen." Lots of people attempt to make a living on the islands and—for a variety of reasons—decide they don't want to live the "island life" after all and head back to the mainland.

Len found odd construction jobs in the still-recessed economy (he's a master carpenter with 35 years' experience under his tool belt) and I looked around for anything that resembled a graphic design job. The best I could find were mind-numbing stints putting together sales flyers for real estate companies.

We also kept our eyes open for a decent place to live, but weren't finding anything.

One day, while perusing Craigslist, Len saw a posting for the sale of an ice cream and cookie shop in Lahaina. I'm a big fan of eating in restaurants, but had absolutely no desire to own or operate one. Len had run his own coffee shop in Prince George, BC, for a couple of years, but gave it up when there proved to be inadequate foot traffic.

We imagined selling ice cream in Lahaina, but decided to give the idea a pass.

Two weeks later, with no permanent jobs and fewer prospects, we saw the ad for the ice cream shop again and decided to check it out. All we knew from the ad was that it was near the famous Banyan Tree and historic Pioneer Inn.

It didn't take much sleuthing to find the right shop. The owner happened to be in that day—one of the two days of the week he worked there—and confirmed it was for sale. He referred us to his real estate agent for the particulars, but at least we knew we had the correct location. Situated on the corner of Front and Hotel Streets, it was a ten-second walk to the Banyan Tree, a thirty-second walk to the harbor, and no walk at all to the Pioneer Inn—we were standing under a couple of its hotel rooms. This place had location!

Then we tasted the ice cream.

It was made by Roselani, a family-owned, Maui-based company, which had been in the biz for over eighty years. It was the best ice cream either of us had ever had. We thought: *Anybody could sell this!*

So instead of buying a house and finding work, we bought our jobs and put the house hunt on hold. We officially became the local sugar-pushers in May of 2013.

The shop was decorated with a traditional woven *lauhala* leaf mats (basically, beige) throughout. It's a nice look, but ubiquitous in Hawaii. I thought the shop could use a splash of color and a new name. The owner had two stores by the same name and we knew an online search would always turn up the original store in Ma'alaea. We decided to call it BanyanTreats since we could easily see the sprawling, 140-year-old, multi-trunked tree from the window and it might give tourists a clue to our location.

We also needed a new logo, something fun, upbeat, kid-friendly but not too childish. We'd seen plenty of geckos hanging around, and one that hung out at the shop seemed a natural mascot. So I put my years of advertising design and fine arts training to work creating a *mo'o* (gecko) logo and began envisioning the interior.

Len helped me construct a twenty foot-wide by four foot-high chalkboard menu, cut in the shape of the banyan tree. Ken, a local sign artist, helped us with our design, printing the color spectrum panel that acted as background to the banyan tree silhouette. We painted the tree with chalkboard paint and I spent two-and-a-half hours every morning for about two months, transferring pencil sketches from tracing paper to the board and using pastels to create the drawings of fruit and other foods denoting each ice cream, shave ice, cookie, and smoothie flavor.

Len put his homebuilding skills to work again, renovating the space in the back of the shop and making other changes we hoped would make workflow more efficient: attaching wheels to the undersides of chest freezers so we could install countertops above, adding cabinets for storage and more workspace, building a dedicated storage area to place the large plastic panels that cover the ice cream at night, and relocating a filing cabinet and employee locker tower.

It was a gamble; two non-restaurateurs taking over a shop during the worst recession we had seen in our lifetime. Just about everything we had was invested in our little ice cream and cookie shop. I thanked the little gecko who watched us from the walls and ceiling as we worked—for they are said to bring good luck.

We scheduled our grand re-opening for September 1, 2013. No one told us it would be one of the slowest days of the year for tourist traffic. There were probably more performers (*taiko* drummers, Hawaiian hula dancers and musicians) than there were tourists that day. But, hey, it had been an ice cream shop for a long, long time and had survived the Great Depression. It had a good track record, right?

If we had any doubts that this was where we were meant to be, and what we were meant to be doing, they were all erased one day when Cindy, the *Taste of Maui* tour guide, showed me and Len a page from her talk about the history of Lahaina.

Exactly 100 years before, a small ice cream and crack seed shop stood in the same location, catering to patrons of the long gone Pioneer Inn movie theater...and the name of that little concession stand?

Len's Sweet Shop.

17

Oliwa's First Lesson at Black Rock

1st place, 2016 Lahainatown Action Committee Short Story Competition

Elaine Gallant

Oliwa jetted across the ocean floor, then scrambled up the aʻa lava wall using all eight of her arms to pull at its crags and outcroppings. After finding a large hole she slipped inside, hoping she'd outrun the heʻe hunter that chased her. And there she waited. When no signs of him appeared, she reached out only to slap an old crab in the kisser as it chomped on a sprig of limu.

"Auwe!" the crusty crustacean cursed. "What's the mattah with you? You got no mannahs?"

Oliwa retracted her arm and yelled from the crevice, "Sorry! But he's still out there!"

"Who's still out there?" he grumbled, clacking his claws in bewilderment.

"The he'e hunter!"

"What he'e hunter? They don't come to Black Rock, only us locals. You gotta be new round here or something."

"I am," Oliwa answered timidly.

"Then come on outtah there and lemme have a good look at you."

Oliwa inched her way forward until she popped from her hole like an untethered balloon bobbing in front of him. She watched as his left eye hooked right and his right drew left, then heard him screech, "Ack! An octopus!" at which she threw a sinewy tentacle over him so he couldn't scurry away.

"Don't eat me!" he shouted.

"Eat you? Why, I need you to look me over."

"What for? You obviously got no broken arms!"

"Because I might be hurt."

"Says who?"

"My mama when she jumped between us and yelled, 'Don't hurt her' and before we got separated... and before I...oh, what am I going to do now?"

"I don't know but you can't stay here 'cause I'm not gonna be your suppah."

"What? I'm all alone and have nowhere else to

go," Oliwa admitted. "If I promise not to eat you or anyone else, may I stay?"

"It's a free world, sistah," the crab grunted. "Now lemme go."

Oliwa released him to a rocky shelf where his crunchy patch of limu grew, announcing, "My name's Oliwa, what's yours?"

"Kala, and I'm plenty hungry, so go away," he answered.

"Me too," she said, making Kala jump. "Not for you, I mean! I gave you my word. So will I see you tomorrow?"

"Tomorrow and the next day and the next. I live here, don't I?"

And she did see Kala again, as well as many other neighbors, who joined them nightly during her inspection and offered helpful advice. First came Elika, the squiggly moray eel, who sympathized with Oliwa but reminded her that everyone feared someone in the ocean. Then came Lui, the big-eyed silver ulua, who suggested she avoid the hunter altogether by going elsewhere to feed. And then there was Momi, the cone-shaped clam, who presented her with a coconut shell, saying all she needed was armor.

Many nights later, Oliwa heard Kala say, "tsk," from under one of her arms and again from under the next. "Tsk" from behind her back and over her head. And then "tsk" to her face as a school of colorful triggerfish, known to them all as humuhumunukunukuapua'a, curiously followed him around in his duties.

Oliwa asked him why he felt so frustrated.

"Seems kinda lolo that you're the only one whose evah seen this he'e hunter of yours," he snapped.

"Perhaps it's because he's not after you," she countered as the humus rallied, "No, no!" "Not after you." "You're only a crab." "A papa'i."

Kala rose up angrily and shouted, "Not aftah me? Why, everybody's aftah me!"

"Not us!" the humus said backing up. "No, sir!" "You're too old!" "Too crabby!"

Oliwa giggled and suggested he join her to see the he'e hunter for himself.

"Okay then, I'll go tomorrow," he answered. "Anyone else?"

Elika, Lui, and Momi nodded excitedly as the humus shivered en masse with delight. "Yes!" "Yes!" "Let's!" "We love an adventure!"

So the next day, Oliwa led everyone to the area where she'd parted from her mother. It wasn't far, just around the corner in fact, but nothing appeared out of order. There were no traps laid, no signs of danger, and certainly no he'e hunter in sight. Even the sun still shone, although it had now painted the heavens a mango-red blush.

Kala clacked as Lui flashed blue in the setting light. Above them, Elika spun in a happy, slow twirl that set her teeth to clattering with delight. Oliwa, meanwhile, kept a vigilant watch amongst the humus. The group "oohhed" and "ahhhed." "How beautiful!" "How lovely!" "And nowhere better than Maui!"

Then without warning, the he'e hunter arrived.

Sppppuuullllaaaash he came, his black hair trailing like a comet and his fingers pointing like a dart. Oliwa was so frightened that all she could do was flatten herself over Kala and pin him to the ocean floor. There she turned the color of its sand, hoping the hunter wouldn't recognize her. But, as always, he came at her.

On his approach, Elika and Lui zoomed out of sight, the humus screamed and scattered, and Momi clamped herself shut.

Oliwa scurried to shore with Kala tucked deep into her underbelly where he pinched her, causing much pain and forcing her three tiny hearts to beat out of rhythm. They went therrump, barrump, katrump.

Once on land, she panted, "Ouch, Kala! That hurt!"

When he didn't respond, she called, "Kala, are you okay?"

And when he still didn't speak, she flipped him over and blew into his face. Soon came a sputter.

"Ack! Ack!" he coughed, spewing black ink from his mouth. "Ack! Ack! Ack!!"

"Oh, Kala, I'm so sorry to have squirted you, but you pinched me."

"On account you were smothering me and now this! Ack, ack, ack!"

"But the he'e hunter! He was there. Didn't you see him?"

"Naw! All I saw was you."

"Well, I was trying to protect you. So forgive me because I didn't mean to, Kala...it's just...it's just..." Her apologetic eyes turned upward to a group of people on the beach dressed in colorful pareos who were singing and dancing with their arms raised toward the setting sun. Looking higher still, she saw a row of torches burning bright along the ridgeline of Black Rock. Then she next saw, coming from out of the water, a proud, young lad who ran to join in the celebration.

Oliwa inched toward Kala only to be halted by

his outstretched claw.

"Is that your he'e hunter?" he asked.

"Yes," she answered softly.

"I see."

"You see what?" she whispered, keeping her eyes fixed on the group ahead.

"I see he's no he'e hunter, Oliwa. He's the one who lights the torches."

"He lights the torches?"

"Uh-huh. And aftah he lights them every night, he jumps into the sea."

"Every night into the sea?" Oliwa asked, understanding as she blinked back tears that welled from the swishing sounds of the dancers swaying and the gentle music that floated back to her on the breeze. She looked tenderly at Kala and said, "Oh, Kala, everyone will think I'm such a fool."

"How so?"

"I'm not sure."

"Listen up, Oliwa, for days you been worrin' about that he'e hunter of yours and turns out he's no hunter at all."

"That's true," Oliwa agreed.

"Bettah than true, and if it were me, I'd be jumpin' over rainbows. So let this be your first lesson at Black Rock, okay?"

Oliwa nodded a "yes" and wiped her eyes.

Kala took hold of another of her arms and pulled her toward the water, suggesting, "Now, we're gonna dry up out here, so how about we go back in?"

Waiting for them were Elika, Lui, Momi and the school of humus who asked all at once, "Are you okay?" "Are you hurt?" "Did you see him?" "Did you see him?"

Oliwa hung her head. "Yes, we saw him and, no, we're not hurt. Turns out he's no he'e hunter at all. He lights the torches, then afterwards jumps into the sea from the top of Black Rock."

"Ohhhh!" they exclaimed. "We didn't know that!" "We can't go out there."

"I'm so embarrassed."

"Embarrassed? Why be embarrassed?" Elika asked. "Didn't I tell you we're all afraid of someone in the ocean? And now that your he'e hunter is no longer a threat, all you really need to worry about is..."

"We know, we know!" the humus interrupted.

"Shush!" Kala commanded as he peered deeper into the ocean and Elika wound her body protectively around Lui.

"We'll give you that lesson another time, Oliwa," he said. "For now, maybe we bettah go home."

26

At that, the sun's final spark lit upon their path to Black Rock where Kala's crunchy patch of limu grew and Oliwa would grow up to learn much more.

And Breathe

Elaine Gallant

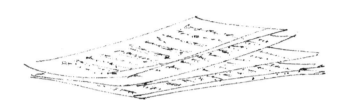

Pauline flipped through a bin of old papers she'd stored since college until her fingers rested on a tender note from David, a mischievous young man with warm, sable eyes and a crooked smile that sat higher on the left than right. The expression, she recalled, had always left her to wonder where his mind had traveled.

She and David had first met during a creative writing class where he'd shown much promise and the two of them had often shared opinions about each other's work. To her, he was cute in that coming-of-age sort of way, although certainly at nineteen years old, a consenting adult. She, however, was thirty-one and married. So she'd suppressed her desire for him even though wild temptations tugged at her heart at seeing his eyes grow wide with undaunted love every time he looked at her. She'd wanted nothing more than to appreciate his affections to avoid any guilt. At least that's what she'd kept telling herself.

Then one day David arrived to class with a ten-page love story he'd wanted earnestly for her to read. As she did, she'd discovered that the entire paper consisted of a single complex sentence. She'd thought it very clever and had told him as much without acknowledging the story's underlying sentiment. Instead she'd felt challenged to shape it into something the professor might better approve. But try as she might, David had been too crafty in his structure, forcing her to give up by the third page and to hand it back to him.

"It's too good," she'd said. "I can't even break it down into something more reasonable. It's a work of art, really, and you've done a masterful job."

He had thanked her and then handed her the note she now held:

You take my breath away. Whenever I think of you, all my words come out in one long stream. I'm afraid to pause for fear that I won't get everything out that I have to say to you. So I thought it might be kind of interesting to put it in a story in the same way. You know? In one long love letter.

She remembered having read the note with her head bent and it was as she'd finished it that David's warm breath had swept closely across her exposed neck. She'd shivered from it and had held her own intake of air. Never had anyone expressed such complete admiration. The memory was remarkable even some twenty years later. She wondered if she would still hold her breath for him if she saw him today.

Pauline placed the note on the nearby table to rub her arms from the thrill the memory gave her and again rummaged through the bin. She was looking for an old collection of inspirational articles that she again wanted to use to conjure up interesting stories for her current writer's blog, a site she'd nurtured for years and had cultivated a large following. Once in hand, Pauline pulled from them a single-spaced narrative titled *And Breathe*. To her surprise, it was a long, complex sentence that read:

Emma wasn't sure but she was fairly certain that time wasn't on her side because love, as she has come to know it, is such a wistful thing that moves always ahead of her just far enough that she cannot grasp it nor can she even tap it on its shoulder where she knows that if she could, it would turn and stop for her like a friend who recognizes her touch and cares deeply enough for her to turn and welcome it because it means as much to her as it does her friend who right at this moment continues to walk briskly ahead by about twenty paces which is just enough distance to keep Emma moving with him as if they are tied by a rope that stretches the distance they share that for at least most of her life up to now hadn't begrudged her any lack of affection except from Kevin, who while in college, promised her the world and then only took hers with him when he left her for Colleen, the one person who knew how deeply she cared for Kevin and who, in hindsight, probably used her to take him away from her which if given even an ounce of thought would be considered a blessing now that Kevin and Colleen are married with three children and looking at a divorce because even Colleen couldn't keep him happy, such is the wandering eye he has particularly on that one day in a burst of spring air when he spotted Adrianne as she ate her lunch of an egg salad sandwich while sitting on a park bench under a giant gum tree that cast heavenly shadows on her very luminous face, one that most men couldn't resist not even Kevin after he gazed at her for over fifteen minutes on his way to work at Bishop, Brown, and Watson, a law firm that specializes in real estate litigation and that was currently pursuing Adrianne's ex-husband for one million dollars in debts that the husband, Bryan, walked away from to Bermuda, a place Kevin would never get to see in spite of the fact that he and Colleen had once agreed to go there to renew their marriage vows but instead ended up separating at the airport after an argument at the ticket counter over seating that proved so upsetting to Kevin that he lashed out at Colleen when she told him to just "drop it" even though he felt he was right to say what he said which pretty much guaranteed both him and Colleen a very uncooperative agent who just this morning had found out that his youngest son was flunking fifth grade, something he himself had done and lived with embarrassingly all his life without ever telling even his wife of fifteen years who probably would have understood and not cared so much, an admirable trait of hers and a reason why he'd married her in the first place on a sunny Sunday back on Maui when the hibiscus were in bloom and the promises of all their tomorrows were ahead of them much like Emma's elusive pursuit of love that she will never really catch up to because love is like one of those complicated yoga moves where you sit with one leg twisted over the other while an elbow presses it back so that when you turn to look behind you, it gives a great squeeze on the kidneys which is plenty enough to make you want to pee until the instructor concludes with, "and breathe."

Pauline read the story over and over, wondering if she'd written it. She couldn't recall exactly, but surely if she had, she must have written it with David's creativity in mind. Besides, who else would have penned it? Also some of the lines and names seemed familiar, yet she still couldn't put her signature to it. So what should she do? The writing would work well for her site and it might even inspire someone else to write a complex one-sentence story. But she'd be a plagiarist if she credited herself given that she wasn't certain she'd authored the piece.

After much thought, she went to her computer and in a tribute to David, posted it as "Author Unknown", along with a full exposé of the young man she'd once been tempted by in college. She then sat back with her eyes closed for a long, long time until the vision of David's love-filled stare dissipated and a deep, warm breath escaped from the crooked slant of her own smile.

A Day with Madame Pele

Elaine Gallant

A thick, white fog billowed up, crisp and fresh, as if carried upon the breath of Madame Pele from the deep blue sea at Hana and scrubbed clean across the volcanic crater at Haleakala. Its absolute pureness tickled our noses. Its chill goosed our skin.

The six of us women hadn't expected her exhale to land so heavily upon our faces, our arms, and our hands. So we just stood there at the crater's rim taking great gulps of it, like hungry koi at a water's edge, and returned it. At eight thousand feet above sea level, this gift of *ha* (breath) with the goddess of fire was humbling.

It was Sharon who broke our communion with

Pele by saying, "Okay, *wahines,* take in the view. It's one of the best!"

"What view?" Ellen asked through the gossamer haze.

"I can't see a thing!" Allyson squealed the obvious.

And then from Meredith, her delivery dull, "Is it always like this?"

Uncontrollable giggles broke loose as Sharon took large swipes with her hands to clear the clouds. It was palpable, our laughter, because here we were—mothers, wives, aunties and tutus—acting like gleeful teenagers skipping school instead of mature adults needing to better assess the situation. All we knew was that our common athleticism would carry us down into the crater and our collective companionship would see us through. Or so we thought.

The giggles stopped when Sharon suddenly disappeared over the invisible edge of the crater onto the trail and I followed like a link in a cascading chain. My intent was to not lose her. I liked Sharon. She was kindhearted and vested in everything she did. She was passionate, as we all were, about things she loved: her husband and family, her pets, the arts, and the greater world around her. She carried an inner beauty that captured my immediate attention, as mine must have for her, because we'd become quick friends.

Behind me shuffled Allyson, who clipped her heavy boot on a piece of volcanic scree.

"Careful," I urged as the firm stomp of her step landed. Solid as a rock, Allyson. Good character and accepting of the consequences for dragging her feet instead of lifting them. She was adaptable, loving and loyal.

Last came Meredith, Kristin, and Ellen, who'd stopped to take photos of the trail's two signs. The first read: HALEMAUʻU TRAIL HEAD, and the other: HOLUA 3.9, KAPALOA 7.7, PALIKU 10.2.

With Holua as our destination, and keeping in mind that the climb up would take longer than the trek down, it meant our "four-to-six-hour strenuous hike" would have us back to the parking lot no later than three in the afternoon and home by early evening, depending on which side of the island one lived. For Meredith and me, that meant after five p.m., but we were up for it.

As Lahaina neighbors, we'd hiked other trails before, finding one another resilient, determined, and focused on the job at hand. Her only quirk, in my opinion, stemmed from a lack of inflection in her voice that left her sounding bored. But she wasn't and I liked her for it, because when she laughed, her face cracked sideways to reveal the caring heart she hid.

She'd bolstered me by trusting my ethics and stamina, my outdoor knowledge and experience. She admired my easier attitude and generosity, proven early in our relationship when she needed a pair of hiking shoes and I'd lent her my most comfortable pair. Come to think of it, that next day was the first time I saw her face crack. She'd driven up behind me on my morning walk to notice my hobble and the large, white bandages on both heels.

"No way," she stammered as we burst into peals of laughter that renewed every time we thought of it. Funny girl that Meredith, if you dug deep enough.

As for Kristin and Ellen, I hardly knew either, but they appeared likable. Kristin floated with the all-knowing serenity of a yogi, while Ellen, reserved and reflective, often caused me to forget she was bringing up the rear. A dangerous situation under certain circumstances but of lesser concern given this well-maintained path. Plus she had Kristin for company. All told, we were a capable group and once having begun our descent, fell into an easy step.

The sun broke through the mist halfway down the trail to reveal amber and green, gold and orange *'ama'u* ferns that Hawaiians once used to stuff pillows and mattresses. Further away, red-berried *'ohelo* bushes, favored by Hawaii's state bird, the endangered *nene,* grew in abundance. Our cameras snapped. Our fingers pointed. And then, as if Madame Pele decided we deserved more, she revealed the previously hidden view below. The crater's floor was vast and swept clean. Barren. But we knew better, for Maui's heart pulsed in Haleakala's grasses, shrubs, and insects. Its backbone jutted with mossy knobs and rib-like ridgelines. Its spirits lingered in the still rising mist to dance around giant calderas that pocked the landscape. It took our breath away to witness such magic.

Suddenly we were flying down the trail and once at Holua Cabin, unpacked eagerly to refuel and chatter about all we'd seen and still wanted to see. We explored dormant lava tubes alive with story. We examined the fine sand, its color, and texture. We laughed and raised our arms to the demigod Maui. And to Pele. To ourselves. We felt gifted by what Haleakala offered. It was magnificent. But Madame Pele's call to climb soon rang, so we packed and moved off.

Meredith took a rambunctious lead with Kristin and Ellen in tow, while Sharon, Allyson, and I dallied. We talked of future trips and overnight stays until Allyson suddenly sat down.

"I don't feel well," she said, placing the back of her hand across her forehead.

"How so?" I asked.

"I feel faint. Dizzy. I'm out of breath."

I looked up the trail at the other women who didn't look back, so focused they were on their footing, and cursed myself for not yelling to them to return. There's a code to hiking when part of a group suffers and, if there was ever a time to implement it, it was now.

But Allyson insisted she'd be alright. Soon. Very soon. All she needed was to sit a while.

Sharon and I exchanged glances. Hers said, "This could turn bad." Mine said, "Let's hope not because there's no way the two of us could carry her four miles uphill."

So again I looked to the other women only to have them look back, make some comments between one another, and march on. *What? They would intentionally leave us down here? Was it my imagination? My own worry? Surely not.*

When Allyson finally felt well enough to stand, we braced her on both sides to help her tenderfoot it back onto the trail. It was slow going but hypoxia from Haleakala's thinner, alpine air can be serious. We all knew that, or at least I had assumed.

I felt unsettled, so I did what I always did to calm myself. I kept the conversation going so that none of us, especially Allyson, would dwell on her condition. Sharon spilled one story after another. And as the trail rose, so did our level of confidence. Before long, we were at the summit once again. It had taken us longer than the other women to ascend, but we'd spent the time well.

When we reached the parking lot, they welcomed us with much anxiety, except for Meredith whose eyes landed squarely on me.

"What took you so long?" she blurted.

"We made it, thank you very much for asking," I deflected.

"What does that mean?"

"It means we were in this together and you left us."

"It was getting late and you were taking your time."

"Allyson felt sick."

"Oh." And then she added, "Sorry," which she was; I could tell because her face splintered. I forgave her instantly.

In the end, I suppose it was true that our

athleticism carried us down into the crater, although as hoped, it wasn't our collective companionship that kept us together. Instead, it was our doggedness at the challenge thrown each faction—the ones who needed to feel safe from the trail and those who needed to be safe on the trail.

Regardless, Madame Pele showed us much compassion and released everyone unharmed. She even provided poetic justice by forcing the others to wait since Allyson, Sharon, and I held all the car keys. So I send Madame Pele a grateful *mahalo* for guiding us safely through this day. Her welcoming gift of ha at the start of our journey joined us together unlike any other gift could and in a place no other gift can—deep in the heart of Haleakala's crater.

L.O.V.E.

Lynette Chun

In days of yore when language was evolving from a series of grunts, and acts of tenderness were relegated to hunting and bringing home a successful catch, there were no words to express emotions and feelings. Such it was—a daily routine in the life of a young husband and wife—if we could even label their relationship by such terms. In their time, there were no rituals for bonding. Centuries later, the term would be "shacking up." Being with her, and only her, was a very serious matter to this young man, burly and gruff in nature.

Still a nomadic society, all males hunted. The

meat was dressed on-site. Deer were fast, but—skilled with the bow and arrow—the young man was faster, and he always made a clean hit with one arrow.

All females were expected to prepare the meat for consumption in some way—cook it, dry it, smoke it. If the meat were left to age for several days there was a definite tangy flavor. She knew nothing about cooking and simply boiled the venison. He ate it day in and day out to show his appreciation for her efforts. Needless to say, there was leftover meat day after day. It never daunted him. He ate and ate leftover venison.

Many snickered and thought he was daft in the head for standing by her. Others saw her as hapless and hopeless.

In time, his devotion earned him the affectionate title "Left-Over Venison Eater." The initial letters, L.O.V.E., became what we call *love,* the reflection of tenderness, caring, and sacrifice.

And that is how the word love came to be.

The Headless Boy

Lynette Chun

The headless boy. Not headless, really. His head and spine had curled inside the cavity of his chest. There was no name for this condition. In every other aspect he was normal.

Doctors couldn't operate, the procedure would have killed him. They wanted to observe him, but his parents refused the inhumanity of it all, and took him home to spend whatever time they could have with their son. They took turns feeding him intravenously, changing his diapers, soothing him, talking to him, reading to him, assuring him of their love.

His parents were his first teachers. They were

his eyes and ears. They brought the outside sensory world to him. Yes, he looked odd as he grew, the head pushing forward like a bump in his chest. His parents knew he was special, but what they couldn't have known was just how special.

When Mother Nature makes a mistake, sometimes she compensates. What they couldn't have known was that even as a baby, he communicated his needs through telepathy. When they thought they were anticipating his baby needs, he was actually communicating without language. He learned language through their constant efforts to teach him. Later, when they imagined he was talking to them, he actually was—telepathically.

When he was thirteen, his parents decided to send him to summer camp for extraordinary and special teenagers.

That was when he met *her.*

She was precocious and extremely loquacious—talking all the time. She scooted up to him and sat quietly. He could sense her presence. He was a calming influence. He sent thoughts to her. She answered out loud, as if talking to herself, and he was able to read those thoughts in his mind.

She had no legs—not even stumps. Her biggest wish was to get up off the ground and feel what it would be like to twirl and run and feel the wind rush through her hair.

She had been a guinea pig for new advancements in prosthetics, but her small torso couldn't manage the cumbersome material. This was a time before the development of light-weight microchip technology. She decided she was born without legs, so she would live without them.

He liked her fearlessness. He said he would carry her on his back and twirl her so she could feel the wind in her hair. She said she would be his eyes and ears. They became inseparable and knew they were meant to be together forever. They wanted to share their special love and start a family, but they knew that he wouldn't be able to carry her on his back if she were pregnant.

They devoted themselves to each other in perfect harmony. Minutes, hours, days, weeks, months— time itself measured their steadfastness. You can still see them today, years later, sitting side by side. She looks as if she is talking to herself, when in reality, she is having a conversation with him. The pattern has never changed from the day they met.

Mother Nature often makes mistakes. Sometimes the unexpected results can be much more than she anticipated.

Mother's Daughter

Lynette Chun

I AM my mother's daughter,
Stubborn, strong-willed,
Recalcitrant, resilient, outspoken,
Curious, yet cautious, spunky, adventurous,
Emotions hidden.

I am NOT my mother's daughter,
At ease with different strata of the social milieu,
Unfashionably fashionable,
A believer in multiculturalism, whatever that is,
Thin-skinned when criticized, insecure,
Emotions on view.

My mother taught me to try everything once before deciding whether I liked it or not. That's a good rule when it comes to food, except for sunny-side up eggs. I could outlast her at the table when there was toast and an egg with a runny yolk, or a soft-boiled egg in one of those fancy little eggcups. How can anyone eat and slurp slimy raw egg yolks? I can even taste the egg in vanilla ice cream or yellow cake. Thank God for chocolate. Make it dark chocolate while you're at it. My taste has matured.

Trying everything once is not such a good thing when it comes to drugs and sex. I'm glad I didn't like cocaine or maryjoanna (you know what I mean) or hashish, and was too scared to try that little blue dot.

Mom and I never talked about the facts of life. I had my first menstruation at age ten. Most girls in the tropics do. We'd giggle at that long word that others called the curse, or monthly, or period. Period.

I AM my mother's daughter,
Caring, generous, thoughtful,
Giving, almost selfless beyond self.

I am NOT my mother's daughter,
I want to divorce my dys-not-so-fun-tional family,
Break tradition, live my own life by my own rules,
Bear responsibility for me alone.

My mother taught me to look past the tip of my nose, in other words, go beyond my island boundaries, seek education and opportunity. She told me I had a mouth. Use it to ask questions. Don't just stand there and look stupid or expect others to do my work for me. This doesn't help when it comes to today's technology. Nobody really talks to anyone anymore. I'm expected to tap-tap-tap a question or an answer. What happens when I'm stuck and technology doesn't know that I don't know shit?

I AM my mother's daughter,
Other people matter, their opinions, too.

I am NOT my mother's daughter,
 Other people don't matter; what they do or think
   is their decision.
I'm selfish, I will not relinquish my autonomy.

My mother grew up during the Great Depression. She says it is here again. Better save your money.

I splurged and spent forty dollars for lunch on a Crab Louis salad. It was over the top, I admit, but that was what I wanted. My philosophy is "Food Before Friends." You only live once. Choose your splurges.

I AM my mother's daughter.
I AM my own person.

Weeds

Lynette Chun

I'd like to be a weed that can grow anywhere,
   anytime, anyplace.
I will be hardy, resilient, tenacious.
My needs will be simple.
Enough water, light, and bare nutrients.

No one has to tend to my well-being.

I will germinate from a tiny seed from wherever
   I am.
I will sprout, meander, and seek my way into life-
      giving source.

A weed most definitely be
From seed dropped,
Grow here, there, anywhere,
Is as good as good is for me.
Meander, sprout, seek illumination out of darkness,
Find sustenance and nurture along the way, simple
    needs, hardy, resilient, tenacious.

Weeds get clipped if they grow through a rock wall,
Pulled out if their presence shatters the illusion of a
    still life garden,
Poisoned if there are too many.

My fervent wish for you and all the world is to
    embrace being a weed,
to see beauty in the not-so-beautiful,
to care for the misfit, live and let live.

Weeds grow in my head.
I pull them out or the tangled roots muddle
    clear thinking.
But why should my thinking always be clear?
I follow not my own life instructions of allowing
    weeds to have their space,
of not being neatly manicured.

What are weeds anyway?
Are they the reminders that life isn't always what it

seems to be,
the itch that needs to be scratched,
the anger that turns into cancer,
the knife blade that beheads,
the gun that shoots,
the helping hand in a flood,
the text message that says,
"Have a great day, I love you."?

I am a weed.
Independent. Resourceful.
No one need tend to my well-being.
I don't take much space, only what is allotted to me
    to grow, bloom, and maybe flower.
I mind my own business,
I'm a good neighbor.

Want to be my friend?

Will You?

Lynette Chun

If I can no longer speak, who will be my voice?
If I can no longer see, who will be my eyes?
If I can no longer hear, who will listen for whispers
    from angels?
If I can no longer stand, who will stand up for me?
If I can no longer feel my heart beat, who will tell
    my story?
Will you?

Old?

Lynette Chun

You know when you're old,
White hairs in your nostrils, on the chin, above
    the lips,
Down by the pubes, under the arms,
Where else? The eyebrows, too? Oh, spare me.
Time for permanent bed. No, don't want to go.
Read me more stories, tell me more tales.
I've lived them, you know,
But I like to hear them told.
Because I'm old.

My mind's still sharp. I can think for myself.
Can't get around too well, so a walker I must
  use.
I know I'm old, you don't need to remind me,
As I've said before, I've paid my dues.

My card has expired? No way.
You'll have to take me kicking and screaming.
DNR? Ha! Do Not Reincarnate.
I'm one-of-a-kind, you see.
They broke the mold after they made me.
Do I need to remind you, I'm precious.
And quite old.

I leave you now of my own free will.
Why, you ask? Because you don't even listen.
My stories are a bore, you say I repeat.
When my voice has been stilled, you'll wish
  you took time
To appreciate my jokes, laugh at my rhyme.
Because, my dear, quite frankly, it's the end of
  the line.
Sweet dreams and good night.
Don't let the bed bugs bite.

As iBrush my hair

John Noah Hoʻomanawanui

As iBrush my hair...
iAm Blessed to be in Haʻikū
.
Haʻikū
Amidst her flaws
Beckons
old-timers & newcomers alike
A community hidden on
The mauka side of Hāna hwy
Upstaged by her kitschy sister,
Paʻia & verdant sister, Hāna
Yet, her strands of hair
Sets her apart

And
Are aptly named;
Kauhikoa, Kaupakalua,
Kuiaha Komohana (West),
Kuiaha Hikina (East)
Kokomo, Pēʻahi...
If you are able to untangle
Each strand
And weave through them
Or braid them
As i
By riding
Walking or running
Even swimming
Her flaws
diminish
.

Haʻikū
Amidst her flaws
Feels for her own
Five months ago,
Our petrol proprietor
Ralph
Lost his wife, Lenette
Unexpectedly
.

As soon as iWas able
iFlew on my moped

To hug. To squeeze his hand.
iHad to wait my turn
For there were others
Who felt the same
As i
For Ha'ikū feels for her own
Last Monday
Greeted by our
laundromat's proprietors
Isaac & Uncle Andrew
A son & father combo
iFinished my laundry
A few days later
Isaac passed
Unexpectedly
Uncle Andrew seems to be holding on
And promptly runs the laundromat
Through the wave of compassionate
    visitors & patrons
Ha'ikū
Feels for her own
Tangled w/ sadness & hope
Her hair is her Glory
.

Ha'ikū
Amidst her flaws
Beckons

Lather, Rinse & Repeat

John Noah Hoʻomanawanui

Stowed away
Beneath the wave's foam
(Its length
Quarter of a mile
Fr the shore to the horizon
Its width
Fr the lil' cove
At Mama's Fish House
To Turtle Bay)
Holds a mystery
Echoed in
The wave's arrival
On the jagged shoreline

.

Held as white socks
To my feet
iGlide
The crest

.

White foam,
Mesmerizing as
Cotton fields
White wash,
Refreshing as snow

.

Do you hear?
Do you see?
The treble
Swirling

.

My head enters
The foam,
Immersion
A depth
A tone
Known
To Neptune

.

Aquatic song

.

Do you see?
Do you hear?

.

Tomorrow
The foam
Will have faded

.

The treble remains
Swirling

.

My hair, the bass washes
My hair, the treble untangles
The melody
Styles my hair's flow
The lyrics
Protect its secrets
Behind its sheen

.

Fr my nape to my crown
A depth
A tone
Known
To Neptune
Stowed away
Beneath the wave's foam
Ku'au

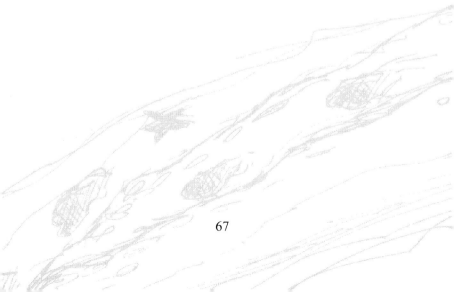

Bus Vignette #13

John Noah Hoʻomanawanui

Eyes opened
fr my nap
W/ Your gentle curves
uLay beside me
Aura of blue
Above thee
As a halo

All transgressions
And lies transfigurations
Fall slack

And helpless
Around thee
.

uGlide across
The window pane
Bronze curves in motion
Tho' in repose
As a Diana Hansen-Young
Painting
In the nude
.

The white muʻu
(Usually depicted in her art)
instead,
suspended above
Your azure aura
Fancy
iShould open
My eyes
& see you
.

Haleakalā,
My eyes
Dare not blink
As iYawn

'Īlio'oPi'i, Kalaupapa

John Noah Ho'omanawanui

20/20 Kahuina
Each night...
20yards fr the place where iLay my head to rest each
night, others lay in their eternal rest.

20yards from their green waves of grass, monk seals
frolic in the blue waves.

20yards from these mammals' leisure, black tip
sharks patrol the warm tide pools.

Recent mornings...
iAwake & walk 20 yards to pay my respects.

Awe-inspired, iThen swim in the waves hearing a
seals' belch less than 20 yards away.

Aware, iWade in the tide pools while the young
manō tickle my feet as they swim past. iSat for an
hour, until one disappeared and returned, it seems,
w/ Mama shark.

Richard's Salad

Jo Ann Carroll

My friend Richard, I've forgotten his last name, sauntered into Whalers Bookstore, carrying a bag of vegetables to make a salad. He made sexy salads. The store had all the equipment he needed, it had once been an Upstart Crow book shop on the third floor of the Wharf Cinema Center. It had refrigerators, a stove top, microwave and a coffee-maker along with books and donuts. He set his bag of ingredients on the counter, found the sharpest knife, and started chopping. "Hey. Jo Ann, take a look at these." He handed me several photographs.

"See the guy on the end?"

"Yes."

"He says he famous. Do you know who he is?"

"Yes," I laughed. "I know who he is."

"Not me," he said as he slashed a big ripe tomato.

Richard and his girlfriend and a man and woman stood together, arms around each other's waist. Richard wore tan trunks and each woman had on a bikini, the fellow on the end wore a suit and tie and shiny black shoes.

"Who took this picture?" I asked.

"His chauffeur."

Richard had been a math instructor at MIT. One cold winter afternoon he walked out of his classroom, locked the door, left the key in the lock, hitched a ride to Logan airport, and bought a one-way ticket to Maui. He established an abode in a cave on the ocean side of the pali and lived there for fifteen years. He was an avid tennis player and made money on the beaches in Lahaina photographing young couples holding hands at sunset.

"So, Richard," I asked, "what did you think of this guy?"

"Full of himself but he paid good. I was his guide for three days. We did the island. He liked to eat and talked a lot.

"How did you meet him?" I asked.

"I was sitting on the beach, in Hana, drinking a beer, and watching my girlfriend body surf. Next thing I know this guy is sitting next to me slapping me on the back. Starts yakking at me. He said: 'See that woman out there in the water?' "

"Yeah." I said.

"I made her famous." Gave me another whack.

"Did you ask how he made her famous?"

"Sure I did." Richard laughed. "The guy said: 'I got her pregnant.' Then he slapped me again. You want the pictures?"

I took them, got some rubber cement, and glued them to the end of a bookcase where they remained for years, until someone stole them.

Back in the eighties I had observed this same man at a breakfast meeting at a book convention in Las Vegas. The authors speaking that morning were T.C. Boyle, John Updike, Angela Lansbury and our fellow in the photos.

"That guy wrote a book?" Richard asked with a silly smirk on his face. That man really wrote a book?"

"So he says. Claims to have written several."

"Jeez, Jo Ann, that's hard to believe."

"T.C. Boyle spoke first, followed by John Updike, then it was Angela Lansbury's turn to speak. She had written about nutrition and exercise. As she was speaking and recapping her high points, the fellow in the photo leaped to his feet, put both hands on her shoulders and pushed her down into her chair. It got nervously quiet in the room. He announced to the audience that she was cutting into his time and his book was more interesting."

Richard has since moved to Colorado, where he earns a living singing on a scenic turnout on I-70. The Whalers bookstore closed in '95 but I'm still hanging out in bookstores, and the fellow in the photographs? What's he doing now? Well, he's the President of the United States, Donald Trump.

Doctor's Visit

Jo Ann Carroll

Yesterday I took Lowell to Dr. Powell's office, a neurologist, to determine what was ailing him. After going through the registration process we headed to the lone elevator. We stood in front of closed doors and stared.

"I don't see a button, there's nothing to push," I said.

Lowell scratched his head. "Yeah, nothing."

I felt a large presence next to me, holding a cane. He used the end of the cane to press a tiny white spot on the right side of the stainless steel elevator. The doors opened. We entered.

"Where are you two from?" asked Foghorn Leghorn, dressed in black shorts and a black t-shirt. Standing at least six feet, eight inches tall, he twirled his cane.

"Lahaina," I said.

"That explains it, you don't get out much, do you?"

"What?"

"You don't know how elevators work. I live in Kihei. Only good thing about Lahaina is you got a Costco Discount store."

"It's only good for TV's, convection ovens and bicycles." I told him.

"What? No produce?"

"No, no produce."

The elevator opened onto the sixth floor, where we had more papers to fill out. When Lowell was called, I was left alone in the waiting room with Foghorn. He resumed talking about Costco. I told him I shopped at Foodland where the prices change hourly.

He laughed, "Ah yes," and smiled, "another example of America's failing capitalism. I used to be the number one salesman to Safeway in the northwest—Seattle—sold Dr. Pepper, Canada Dry, everything except Coke and Pepsi."

I told him, "I used to love Dr. Pepper, but I don't drink soft drinks anymore."

"You're right. They're bad for you, loaded with sugar, they'll kill you.

"James, my name is James, nice to meet you." He leaned forward, chin on the top of his cane, white legs spread wide apart, his big head was all smiles, his long pointed nose bobbed up and down as he spoke. "Like I said, I was 'numero uno' sales rep in Seattle, made a lot of money, had everything I wanted, then boom lost it all, my wife ran off with another man, took our daughter with her. I was devastated. Heartbroken. But I gathered up the pieces of my life and moved to a trailer camp, and there I met a woman who wanted to live on Maui, so we pooled our resources and we bought a little jungle house in Kihei."

"I'm glad for you," I said.

"Then she had a stroke and she was sent to a hospital on Oahu, I went to visit once a week, she was miserable, she wasn't getting any better, went on for six months, she was barely able to talk, she wanted out, so you know what I did?"

"I can't wait to hear," I said.

"I stole her, just picked her up and walked out with her in my arms, no one paid any notice, got her home, put her in bed and there she stayed. I took good care of her."

"Did you get in trouble, did they come after you?"

"Oh, hell yes. One morning we are watching TV and there was a banging on the door, cops and two doctors, said she should be in hospice. I'm her hospice. That's when I realized I was a happy man, I was doing something for someone else, someone I guess I loved, so I told them I was going to keep her and I did. They said she was going to die. Well, that was obvious and she did die while watching *Casablanca,* a nice peaceful death."

"Wow, what a story," I thought.

He stood and stretched. It was like watching a ladder unfold. He sat again and continued, "I've had three back operations and I have terminal cancer and those damn doctors think I should have hospice care. Hell, I'm not that close; besides my daughter arrived last week with her boyfriend. She's planning a wedding in August, wants me to walk her down the aisle. Glad to do it but I've got to talk to her about her fiancé."

"You don't approve?" I asked.

"He's a nice guy but he's a thirty-two-year -old, unemployed, tobacco-chewing log roller from

Oregon. He's got three kids and two ex-wives.

"James," called the nurse.

"James," again louder.

He stood, bowed and said, "Isn't life great?" He had to duck to go through the doorway.

"Yeah, life's great."

Life at the Astro Motel in Pasadena

Jo Ann Carroll

Freddy Sanders arrived at eleven thirty on a Friday night. He drove a long black car two shades darker than his skin. He filled out the check-in form, paid twenty dollars, gathered up his key, tipped his stingy-brimmed hat, bowed and left the lobby. I watched as he drove to his parking space. He got out, opened the trunk, and unloaded six suitcases.

"Yikes," I thought, "he only paid for one night." The right rear door opened. Two tall black women in short skirts, clunky high heels, cropped tops, and sparkling earrings slithered out of the back seat, more like unfolded. They stood in the parking lot, rubbed their eyes, laughed, did a couple of bump and grinds against the car. It reminded me of my old dancing days. That's when I saw Freddy's name in gold script on the back fender.

He said something and, quick as a blink in the night sky, the women gathered the suitcases and carried them to the room.

Freddy followed. He paused at the door and looked around.

I thought to check if anyone was following him. Into the room the three of them went. They closed the curtains.

I turned on the NO VACANCY sign, locked the front door and went back to bed.

In the mornings we served coffee and donuts in the recreation room by the pool, next to the sauna. That day after the usual morning business, Freddy strolled into the office.

"I'd like to pay for a week in advance," he said.

"Sure. How'd you like the room?"

"Groovy."

He set his coffee and donut on the counter.

"I'll have to charge you for an additional person." I said.

"Two additionals," he said. He handed me a roll

of hundreds that he pulled from his skintight bell-bottom pants. "Take what you need," he said, as he drained his coffee cup. "Good coffee."

"Thanks," I said as I handed back his wad of money.

"Laters," he saluted with his donut.

His two black panthers were waiting for him, each wearing short shorts, with big clunky high-heels. They waved, Freddy got behind the wheel, and the black beauties settled in the back seat.

The weekends were a different clientele than the Monday through Friday residents. Pasadena was an early high-tech location, before Silicon Valley. We had lots of commercial men for the week; on the weekends they left to explore other parts of Southern California. They returned Monday nights to resume their research and development. Friday and Saturday were predominately "quickies" as we called them. Illicit activity was entertainment for us.

Freddy stayed a month. I got to know him and "his girls" as he referred to them.

He was their pimp; he dressed the part. I was approached by the tourists and asked, "Who is that negro man? What is he doing here?"

I'd take the questioner into my confidence and explain that he was a famous basketball player. In those days if you were black, you were either an athlete or a criminal.

"Please don't ask for his autograph."

They were impressed and left him alone only to smile when he passed them in the parking lot.

This was in the days of telephone switchboards. When a guest made a call, the board would ring and we put the call through, requesting time and charges to be added to the guest's bill.

One day, Freddy called his mother, and I heard her say, "Don't come home. You're wanted for murder in Detroit." She cried,"My baby, my baby."

His girls slept late. By the time they were up and about, the commercial men were gone and tourists types were either at Santa Anita or on a tour of Hollywood's movie stars' homes.

A couple of days a week they brought their new shoes to the office for me to try on. I'd get them on, straps, rhinestones, buckles, and high heels. "How do you walk in these things?" I wobbled and tottered around the office. They giggled and rolled their eyes at my struggles.

"Honey, you got the legs but you ain't got the walk."

"You like your work?" I asked as I freed myself from the stilettos.

They laughed, lightly punched each other, rolled around on the pale blue office couch, kicked their long black legs in the air, flailed their arms over their head, bracelets and earrings jangling.

"I'm serious," I said.

They laughed louder. "Come on, honey girl, you be serious," growled a panther, as she flashed a menacing set of ivories.

They were our quietest guests and the least trouble. Freddy sat in the rec room, read the *LA Times,* and drank coffee.

Mr. Bogan sat across from him reading the racing form. He was a professional gambler and writer for *The Andy Williams Show.* He and his wife, and his wife's nurse, Elizabeth, were in room 217, the largest suite; three double beds overlooking the swimming pool.

Mr. Bogan was in his mid-to-late fifties, a florid Irishman. His wife was ninety and had stooped round shoulders. Her elbows rested on her knees when she stood, which wasn't often. Mr. Bogan and the nurse were having an affair. Lucky for them, Mrs. Bogan was nearly blind and deaf. One afternoon as I was trying on the panthers' shoes, I got a call from room 217.

"Jo Ann, I need your help, I have to give Mrs.

Bogan a bath."

My first thought was "why call me?"

"I can't do it alone."

"OK, I'll be up."

The Panthers gathered their shoes and went back to room 107 to watch *As the World Turns.*

When I got upstairs to their room, the door was standing open. Mrs. Bogan was sitting on the end of the bed closest to the small bathroom, nude. Nude, not a hair on her body except for a long black braid that hung down to her waist.

Nurse Elizabeth was a bundle of nerves. "What's the problem?" I asked.

"She doesn't want a bath, says she's too old. She's a stubborn old biddy."

"OK, how often do you bathe her?"

"This'll be the first time; Mr. Bogan said she's getting crusty."

You might think getting a ninety-year-old into a bathtub would be easy, but you don't know what to grab hold of that won't puncture you or put your eye out.

The bathroom was tight, a toilet and an over-sized tub.

Nurse filled the tub, I picked up Mrs. Bogan and carried her to the tub. She squirmed and wiggled. I staggered about like I was auditioning for a *Three Stooges* remake.

Plop into the tub.

Nurse Elizabeth, the mistress, lathered Mrs. Brogan a little too much, so we had a hard time holding on to her as she bobbed up and down.

"I think she's clean. Let's get her out and dried off."

It was difficult getting her into the tub but even harder getting her out. We drained the tub and after many failed attempts, Nurse grabbed Mrs. Brogan by her braid and gave one humongous yank.

She was out and on the floor.

I picked her up and put her in bed.

"Anything else before I get out of here?"

"No, thank you, Jo Ann."

On my way back to the office I passed room 107. The door was open, I saw Freddy and his girls sitting on the bed eating popcorn, watching *Bugs Bunny* cartoons.

"Come in," they called. "We leave tomorrow."

"Why, where are you going?"

They laughed. "La Jolla, The Del Mar track opens this week."

"I'll miss you," I said. As soon as I spoke I realized I meant it.

"We have something for you. Freddy, get the box under the bed."

He obeyed, handed it to me.

"Open it."

In the shiny white box, and wrapped in pink tissue paper, was a pair of shoes, heels at least five inches, gold and silver straps, rhinestones on the toes. Probably the most garish, whorish shoes ever created.

"I love them." I felt tears well up.

"Yes, they are so you," purred the panthers.

Clouds

Jo Ann Carroll

When I was five and my sister was three, we would lie on our backs on the thick green grass in our front yard and look up into the Parisian blue skies, pre-smog days of Southern California. We watched the clouds.

We saw animals, buildings, and people in those wispy formations. We made up stories to fit the images.

Those were the days when kids played in their front yard without their parents being arrested for leaving children unattended, also those were the days before the construction of the Pasadena freeway, later nicknamed the worlds largest parking lot.

During the summer our family went to the beach every Saturday. We drove to Huntington Beach straight down Pasadena's Rosemead Boulevard, to the oil wells that rimmed the sand.

Sometimes we stopped and picked up our father's uncle and his wife Vivian, who my mother thought was part Chinese because her eyes were tilted upward. "Slanted," she said with a sneer.

Jim and Vivian lived in a quonset hut with two billy goats. They made candles: big, fat, white candles with flowers cascading down their sides. I thought they were beautiful.

For these trips to the beach, mother made hamburgers that she wrapped in waxed paper and put in a pressure cooker to keep warm. We lugged blankets, umbrellas, towels, an ice chest, sun lotion, a radio, and toys.

I remember one afternoon in particular. We ate hamburgers and potato chips and topped them off with an ice cold coke from the metal cooler, while the adults were playing canasta. Jim and Vivian were sitting with their backs to the ocean, and my mother was dealing the cards when a small brown-and-white speckled seal crawled out of the water and waddled up to Vivian and laid his head in her lap. We assumed it was a he because he was attracted to Vivian. She petted him, tickled his chin. He had huge brown eyes and long lashes. He stayed with us all afternoon.

When it was time to pack up, he understood. He watched as we gathered our stuff.

We had to get back to town; our father was part of the neighborhood night watch program. We had to be home before dark. He sat on our roof as soon as the window blinds were secured to keep light from escaping into the dark night. No street lights, and a ten o'clock curfew unless you were on your way to or from work.

He sat with special binoculars, scanning the sky for Japanese airplanes, or was it the Germans that were going to bomb us?

As we trudged across the wide beach carrying our belongings, I looked back, I swear to this day, that little speckled seal raised his flipper and waved goodbye. I have a photograph of the seal and my great aunt in her black two-piece bathing suit, no belly buttons or bikinis in those days.

We clambered into the black Studebaker, all hot and sandy, dropped the relatives at their Quonset hut, the goats bleated "welcome back."

As I was saying about those clouds, that was our television then. On days when the black clouds rolled in and thunder thundered, we thought it was God farting, and the rain was him peeing on us.

I wish I still believed.

First Night on a Maui Beach

Oliver Gold

Moving and retiring to Hawaii is a delicious, bitter-cold cocktail of worry and relief. Sure, there's the dream…tanned girls in bikinis, sunshine and trade winds. But Uncle Ole's first three days on Maui were slapping him awake with habitat scarcity.

Where you gonna live, brah? he wonders as his savings continue to un-save.

He'd been searching the classifieds and Craigslist. All he wanted was a spectacular beach condo with a great view, valet parking, and room service that would fit his budget of six hundred dollars a month.

Holy Coconuts, Captain Cook. Just one night

in a beach condo can cost that much! laments the disillusioned half of his brain.

Told you so, brags the practical side, without any real satisfaction.

When Ole finally surrendered that fantasy, he did find a small, furnished, single room to rent in a big house for eight hundred bucks a month (share the kitchen and bath). It was a few blocks up the hill from Kahana Beach on Maui's west side. Carrying his guitar and three cardboard boxes of personal stuff up one flight of stairs had worn him out. He was in his mid-fifties, it was mid-afternoon, and he needed a nap. But nesting there on his new bed, his internal calculator was keeping him awake, noisily crunching his daily survival budget down from thirty to twenty, then fifteen dollars a day. If his retirement plan of finding a cute, rich widow to marry didn't happen soon, he was gonna have to find a job.

No mo' job, brah, thinks the lazy side of his brain.

Yah, you came here to retire. Just spend your 401(K) carefully, advised the practical side of his cabbage.

He gave up on sleeping; he was hungry but eating was expensive. He unrolled his yoga mat out on the floor of his new room; meditation is free. In three breaths he felt better. After twenty, the twisted worry muscles in his neck were melting like butter on popcorn, a meal he could still afford. He considered his options: Option One, no job. Option Two, volunteer and be patient. He'd already played dinner music at two rest homes. Option Three, make some popcorn.

Toward evening he turned to his other solace, music. Ole picked up his guitar, hugged it with love, and wandered through the *naupaka* bushes down to Kahana Beach. This stretch of Hawaii sand is a tourism postcard of paradise. The surf rolled, the bikinis strolled, the kids tumbled and shouted. He was a retired teacher, trying to reinvent himself as a poet and songwriter, so he hoped. His thoughts waxed large, melting as he viewed a Maui beach up close and hot for the first time. Some of the surf soaked into the sand, some rushed back out into itself leaving the shore wet with golden light from the campfire burning in the western sky. Marshmallow clouds were toasting burnt yellow. He didn't take a rum drink with him, didn't stop at the beach bar–the yoga had done its magic. Relief won out over worry. In fact, his confidence was beginning to hit on seven cylinders, not real smooth yet but revving darn close to a full V-8.

Down the beach he saw a large revival meeting

of sundown worshipers gathering in front of the Valley Isle Resort. Ole headed toward them. As he approached they waved him over, maybe because he was carrying a guitar, maybe because he was projecting love in all directions and they felt it. A tall, suntanned man set down his beer and walked up on the lawn by the palms to fetch a beach chair for him. He seemed friendly until he spoke,

"Here comes another beach bum. You might as well sit down with the rest of the riffraff," he smirked and offered a handshake of welcome. "I'm Jack, this is Bill and Bonnie, that fat guy is Chubby Checker, the skinny guy over there is Tom Hanks, that's Dwayne and Zina, Michael Jordan, Jim and Sue, Captain Kangaroo, Mike and Linda, Lazy Billy Bones and sweet Lorena, Paul and Patti, Dr. Seuss, Steve and Lee Ann, Herman Hess, Al and Diane. The big ugly guy there is my golf buddy Al, his wife Kathy, that's Steve Miller, Bruddha T and pretty Ligia, Dan and dear Marla, Michelle Wei and Sergio, more golf buddies. That's Loopy Denny and his wife Karen, Tom Selleck, Judy and Tim, Rey and Diane, tall Tim and Ella, good old Floyd and Pat. There's Judy, Judy, Grumpy and Lady Smurf, Suzie, Melinge, Carl Sagan. That's Bob Marley, there's Andrea, famous Mike, Jack and Sally, Maui Jim,

Barry and Lindy the happy winos, that's Tommy Bahama…"

"Whoa, Jack," said Uncle Ole. "Yer givin' me a nose bleed. Alohaaa, everybody. My name is Oliver Gold and this is my guitar Coco Lani."

He just made that up to be funny, but when he thought about it, that was a great name for his guitar. Everyone smiled and nodded, smiled and nodded again, and raised their drinks in friendly salute. They were happy sunset worshipers accepting him into their congregation. A few even had drink holders stuck in the sand next to their chairs; obviously, experienced, professional, sunset missionaries.

"It's time; so stop all yer yakking," ordered Jack.

There was a bit of digging as nearly everyone obeyed, reached down into beach bags, and pulled out conch shells. Mother Earth was turning in her slow pirouette, rolling toward the East, away from the sun. In that direction the West Maui Mountains stood bravely in the sun's last brilliant hurrah. They reminded Ole of magnificent giants or maybe the defensive line of the Green Bay Packers. He was a poet now, or so he thought.

"Ahhh," a dozen voices sighed at the incredible blueness of the sky.

Perfect blue became bluer if that's possible, as

one half of the sun began to disappear below the sharp edge of the ocean. The puffy clouds were toasting red, about to ignite. Some of the sundowners started pounding on their shells to knock the sand and geckos out. A few had their conch pressed to their lips, already warming them up with soft hums.

"Watch for the green flash," somebody said.

The earth tipped east; the ocean rose and slowly hid the sun. At that same instant there was a brilliant green spark the size of a pencil tip on the horizon where the sun had vanished. It was the start of tonight and the cue for the sundowner shell band to play.

"See if you can get it right this time," Jack grumped as he swung his can of beer down like a concert maestro with a baton. Ole noticed Jack did not spill a drop of his beer, a professional band leader.

Twenty conch shells moaned their ancient call. It was a cacophony of Polynesian magic and rutting moose warble. Old Bill, Denny, and Bruddha Tom blew for over a minute. Their faces puffed out like three purple plums as they blew their lungs out of air. Their final quavering notes waved away down the beach, jumped into the ocean, and diminished under the surf. There were a few moments of hush as the quiet waves soaked into the beach. Then everyone cheered and clapped for the three conch-blowing champions.

"Wow," whispered Ole.

"I've heard cat fights that sounded better than that," complained Jack.

Everybody laughed. Jack must be the ornery favorite of this crowd. Ligia, Captain Billy, and Lorena began to play their 'ukuleles,

"Somewhere...ova da rainbow...," they sang.

Ole sat down with Coco Lani and joined in. When the song ended, Captain Billy asked, "Hey, Ole. How long you been living on island?"

"Ah hah," said Uncle. "Tree days now, brah," he tried some "pidgin" slang, it didn't sound too wrong.

"Lucky come Maui," said Billy. "Now you sing one song."

Uncle checked the tuning on Coco and sang as sweet a song as any of them had ever heard. It sounded like a happy song, but trimmed with threads of melancholy. Uncle Ole was still a little worried about how he was gonna afford to live in Hawaii with all these millionaires.

"Hana hou," (play one more) said Ligia.

"Okay. One more, but then I want to hear you three sing again."

He sang with his heart in his words, a song as

sweet as the first, and the congregation faced the coming darkness filled with hope and music and booze.

Uncle Ole was about to learn that after sundown in the tropics, there are five to ten minutes of twilight afterglow. It started to happen tonight as the high yellow clouds turned into brass as shiny as Aladdin's lamp. It was spectacular brass, like flashing cymbals in a marching band. The lamp wished itself even brighter, and the genie of Maui nights swung his flaming torch and lit the marshmallows with hungry flames of red and gold.

Then to everyone's surprise, purple ink, perhaps conjured up from ocean kingdoms far away, began to blotter softly down into the sky tainting the once perfect gold. The sky became darker and deeper lavender, and it spread like a purple Midas touch until all the gold "dyed." Within seconds the ocean below mirrored the purple sky; waves crushed the shore like burgundy wine. The contagion spread, purpling the sand and palm trees. The painting was complete when the people on the beach were brushed with purple, as if everyone had turned into aliens from planet Purple-Upitor.

"Ah…"

"Ah…"

"Ah…"

Twenty nearly speechless, purple sun worshipers stood still with purple drinks forgotten in their purple hands.

"This only happens once or twice a year," said Captain Billy. "It's so strange that highway traffic slows to a stop. Little kids drop their bicycles and stare."

"Break da eyes, brah," whispered Ole. "It looks photoshopped, like some kinda postcard."

Too soon, the Black Knight, nemesis of daylight, tipped back his cup and drank all the wine out of the sky. From thirteen billion years ago, starlight became visible again. Ole started to hum a tune that was lighting up the neurons of his mind, *Stars come out one at a time, one at a time...*

Starlight has sound? Both sides of his brain feel confused.

Dis island "broke da ears," brah.

His whole body was humming with the sound from the stars, all eight cylinders were idling smooth. Tonight's evening sunset service was over. The purple-baptized believers had witnessed their solar Jehovah at His best. The crowd began to thin. Lorena took Captain Billy's hand, and they said goodnight to Ole. Lorena gave him a friendly Hawaiian hug. So did Ligia. Bruddha Tom shook his hand. Billy's eyes caught Ole's with mutual understanding; there would be other nights like this.

Jack was the last to leave. He turned to Ole as he finished his beer, "Don't bother coming back. We're looking for a real guitar player."

Ole laughed, not sure how to take this, but Jack was smiling from ear to ear and offering another handshake. In a backhanded way, Jack seemed a likable, weird sorta guy.

So are you, dummy, reminded his mind.

Uncle Ole let his mind tumble with that, but he didn't feel tired or want to go home. He wandered further into his first night on a Maui beach and soon found a soft hill of sand. Uncle eased his old body down in a half lotus and re-tuned his guitar. This delicious night was made for music. He could stay up till dawn if he wanted to. No alarm clock would ring, and no boss would miss him. No boss, no-boss, no-boss. He liked the sound of that so much he might write a new song, a no-boss-a-nova.

It was a night of odd Jack and new friendships and songs. He worked on the lyrics of the song about the stars coming out one at a time. He was a passionate, poet and a fifteen-dollar-a-day millionaire retiree with no boss. He offered a prayer of gratefulness, the ninth prayer today, for this chance to live in Hawaii and find a room close to the beach, nice friends, and purple sunsets. It was all treasure, found at last, unburied and his to enjoy.

"Arrrr!" He belly laughed out loud, feeling like Captain Morgan with fists full of gold coins. Only his new coins were the days and sunsets and starry nights of living in Hawaii from now on...maybe.

Occasional tourists and locals were still walking the beach. They passed twenty feet in front of him, and there was enough twilight to see everyone as passing silhouettes. Romantic couples, parents with kids, seniors with dogs, and just plain weird-looking people with one or two parrots on their shoulders all wandered by in a shadow parade.

Plato would like this, the philosopher side of his brain chips in.

Uncle Ole sent music vibes and aloha along to each person as they walked past him. He loved them all. The beachcombers waded in the surf or left barefoot prints along the wet sand. No one was in a hurry. Some of them stopped to listen to him sing about the stars and then walked on. Some ignored the lone guitar player on the dune. He watched a tall slender woman walk slowly by. She stopped to listen for awhile and then continued on down the beach. He could not see her face, just the shadow of her pleasing figure.

When she came back by again, she walked up the slope and sat down on the sand next to him. She didn't say anything. He smiled and studied her. She was very, very cute.

"Hello, beautiful," he said.

"Hi, handsome," she said.

"What's a pretty thing like you doing in a cheap dive like this?"

"Hah! You need to learn some new pick-up lines, beach boy. Maui is not cheap."

"The beach is free."

They both started laughing. She looked fresh and gorgeous, maybe mid-twenties. She was barefoot, wore black shorts showing lovely long legs and a white t-shirt with no bra under it; a liberated woman. She smelled good, like suntan lotion. Ole noticed perfect full bumps pushing from under her shirt right where they should be. She was blonde, a messy hair blonde.

Maybe she pays to have her mop styled all messed up like that. He didn't know much about women's hair fashions, or care.

Just go with the flow, brah, whispered both horny halves of his brain.

"Play another song for me, beach boy."

"Sorry, I don't play on demand."

"Please," she whined so cute.

"Oh, is that a request this time?"

"Uh huh," she nodded, "pretty please."

"Okay, Pretty Please. I think that's what I'll call you tonight."

He smiled and played "Sweet Leilani" and during the chorus, she snuggled closer so that her bare leg was touching his. His response below his waist didn't surprise him. She was warming him up like a vintage tube amplifier. He sang the sweet song with passion. She hung on every word.

"Now, Pretty Please, you sing one for me."

"Is that a demand?" She smiled.

"Yes."

"Well, too bad for you, I can't sing."

"Nonsense, everyone can sing. Are you too shy?"

"I'm not shy, am I?"

He had to agree. She had come over and sat down close to him; she wasn't shy.

"I can't sing."

Ole was trying to look her in the eyes not at her t-shirt. She was a living doll, by starlight.

"Okay, Pretty Please, sing, 'You Are My

Sunshine' and I'll sing along with you if that'll help."

She didn't answer, so he played a dashing little intro on the guitar and nodded for her to start. Her voice was a car wreck, horrible! It curdled the soft night like moldy sour cream poured in a cup of black coffee. She was absolutely the worst singer he had ever heard. She was worse than Bob Dylan. But Ole played one whole verse and let her finish on her own,

"Please don't ta-ache my sunshieeenie awai-iaaeeiiee-yawl."

"You were right, doll. You can't sing."

"Told you.

"What *can* you do?" He was curious. She was lovely. It was exciting to have a sexy young woman take an interest in him on his first night on a Maui beach.

"They tell me I'm a good kisser," and she gave a shy smile, wetting her lips with her tongue.

Something suspicious was ping-pinging on his chick radar.

"How old are you, Pretty Please?"

"I'm sixteen, almost seventeen next month."

"Yikez, girl!" Ole stood up. "Find a beach boy your own age, not a senior citizen."

Uncle walked away shaking his head, waving his guitar around in fuming frustration.

Life is full of crazy people, brah. You can't always go with the flow, reprimands his brain.

"You told me to go with the flow. I could go with the flow all the way to jail listening to you!"

You should see a psychiatrist, buddy.

"I can't afford psych therapy dumb-ass, remember, fifteen dollars a day?"

You're the dumb-ass.

"No, you are."

Then at least we agree on something.

Ole was surprised at his brain's bad attitude but he didn't feel all that stupid. As he walked along the shoreline, he gazed up at the stars and sent out another prayer of gratitude; the tenth today. He was just one of those guys who dream all their lives of living in Hawaii with hula girls and palm trees.

Down the beach, in the distant darkness, he heard something wild and free and strange. It was a jungle sound he'd only heard in Tarzan movies. He held his guitar close like a lover he could trust, one his own age, and wandered toward the rumble of native drums.

Illegal Beach Fire

Oliver Gold

Somehow Uncle Ole had survived for almost a year on Maui. He was a smiling, fifty-something, retired teacher trying to reinvent himself, volunteering, and playing guitar and singing in bars for a thin living. It was a dream come true, but he was hurting inside. That's the price of loving someone. He'd been married for a long time. It was hard to let go.

He thought of his mother. Moms are experts at letting go. Ole needed her advice. He hit Speed Dial number one on his cell phone. Number one used to be Tanya. Mom was real quiet on the Iowa side of the call as he told her about the divorce. When she finally did speak, her advice was simple, be strong, be kind, be generous. Ole thanked her, said goodbye, closed his clamshell phone, and turned to his second oldest friend, his guitar.

Love's stupid arrows were still stuck in his chest, so he spent the rest of the day sitting on his lonely bed, bleeding from the heart, page by page, through every song in his song books. Fortunately, he still had music and his guitar and his mom. In fact, he'd had them all much longer than his marriage. These past lonely months he'd been sleeping with his guitar; it had Tanya's curves.

You're so pathetic, brah. His inner shrink was an expert at self-sarcasm.

By sunset his chest bones still felt broken, but six hours of singing had him breathing in and out again with less pain. Uncle mixed himself a rum and Coke and drank it down while standing in the middle of the kitchen. He refilled it and this time he tossed in some ice and a chunk of pineapple. Ole watched it float on the surface like a yellow life preserver. Its sunshine looked chilled and uncomfortable there among all those tiny icebergs; about as miserable as his neck and shoulders had been living in too-cold Seattle. So he tipped the medicine back and crushed the pineapple with his teeth. Uncle planned to squeeze the fun out of life, too. Even though that meant living in Hawaii without Tanya.

You're finally getting the picture, stupid. His brain just won't lay off.

He embraced his guitar tenderly and walked outside. The almost-sunset color of the sky was beckoning him to the beach. Ole studied the horizon. The sun looked like it was doing the limbo under long ropy clouds the color of whipped cream. Uncle almost smiled wondering,

Jolly Ol' Sol, how low can you go?

Hawaiian sunsets are good medicine for a broken heart. He wanted to feel happy again, so he yoga-ed down on his favorite rise of sand, ready to be healed by a sky full of color. But tonight his great expectations were soon over. A black shroud of cloud threw itself out from the eastern mountains and covered the beautiful sky. It was getting dark too fast, as if the sun was passing out or maybe dying. Far out on the western horizon the last sails of red suddenly dropped off the edge of the earth. It was over too soon. No magnificent colors, no green flash, no afterglow, no healing medicine. It was a "nothing" sunset. He felt the same way.

You're nobody, whispered Emily Dickenson from the dusty library of his mind.

Ole played some Moody Blues chords on his guitar to match his loneliness. After one verse of "Nights in White Satin" it was a black velvet night. Uncle could sing in the dark so he started to play lost chords of this and that. Some of his strum and pluck blew clouds out over the ocean where they began to disappear into thin wisps of vapor. Shy stars were peeking through the torn ribbons sending him little flint-sparks of hope. It wasn't enough. Verses of hurt came limping out of the bombed-out trench where his heart used to be, and he sent them stumbling along into useless battle with his melancholy chords.

Time had slowed down fast, an oxymoron indeed; like happily living in Hawaii without Tanya. A huddle of hours later all those hopeful stars had stumbled across the black clock face of night and piled up in a worthless heap of diamond chips just west of the Big Dipper. It looked like the dipper was about to sweep them into its cup. That reminded him of an astronomy class he took in college. The professor said that our entire, immense galaxy (one hundred thousand light years across) would fit inside those four stars of the Big Dipper. That's how far apart those four corners actually are. It's a dipper well-named.

Somewhere around midnight or later, a man

appeared, moving in long strides down the beach. It wasn't that unusual to see someone walking out here alone at any hour of the night. But this man did not have that wandering beachcomber walk. He was on a mission. This guy marched with a determined pace and was headed right for where Uncle sat. On guard for self-defense, the guitar player laid down his guitar. As the stranger neared, he was talking in an excited voice, "I see you playing the guitar, brah. This is perfect."

Uncle had never seen this character before. He looked kinda scruffy but not dangerous. He was dressed like a haole surf-dude guy. Maybe he was another retired teacher from Seattle. The stranger was carrying a large backpack over one shoulder. He did not try to shake hands. He just said, "I'm Len. Howzit, brah?"

"Hi, Len. Call me Ole."

"I'm gonna build a campfire on the beach tonight, might as well be here if that's okay with you?"

"Beach fires are illegal on Maui, Len. They dirty up the beach with blackened ash and if you cover them with sand, people burn their bare feet on the leftover coals; bad idea."

"No mess, brah. No *pilikia* (trouble). Watch dis."

Len shut up and went to work. He opened his backpack and pulled out three logs. Each one was a few inches in diameter and a couple of feet long. He propped them up against each other in a small tripod. From where Uncle Ole sat it looked like the Great Pyramid out on the sands of Egypt, only smaller. Next Len pulled out a can of lighter fluid and soaked the pyramid for a whole minute with a fine spray. Then he lit a match.

"Shazam, instant campfire! Let's sing a song, Ole."

It was a magic Maui miracle, a cheery campfire burned brightly in front of them, like a burning bush from the Bible.

"Wanna beer?" Len offered, reaching deeper into his backpack.

"No, thanks. I quit beer fourteen years ago, it was making me fat. Got any rum in there?"

"Sorry, brah. Let's sing."

The two new friends sang every verse of Bob Dylan's "Blowin' in the Wind." When they finished, the silence was so unbearably loud, they sang it all over again. The second time around they sounded better, with more harmony in between the answers in the wind. At the end of the last verse nothing more needed to be said. Dylan knew life would always remain a mystery.

The campfire went out. Len got the lighter fluid can and gave the three sticks another good soaking. He struck a new match, and soon the flames were lightly dancing up the pyramid. The fire burned on through three more songs and went out again. Len squeezed the lighter fluid can until it was empty and gave the logs one more match.

They sang "The Hour When the Ship Comes In," and "Boots of Spanish Leather," and "Hey, Mr. Tambourine Man." When fire left the logs for the third time, it sorta flew up into the night sky like an *'uhane* (a spirit). Black darkness tightened around them with the same shroud that killed the sunset, but the moon was out over the mountains behind them now, lighting the beach with an off-white pallor.

Len reached for the three logs and stuffed them back in his pack. They didn't show any sign of burning, not even too hot to touch. He gathered his empty lighter fluid can, the three burnt match sticks, and his two empty beer bottles into his backpack, zipped it shut, shook Ole's hand, and said goodnight. Then he turned away with that same determined walk and disappeared down the beach. Ole looked down at the sand in front of him, no ash, no coals, and no mess.

"I like this island," he whispered to nobody.

His worry and heartache were forgotten. He actually felt okay. In fact, as soon as he admitted he felt better, he was almost happy again. Then, like a karmic reward for getting over himself a "moonbow" of pastel colors began to shimmer in the clouds above Molokai island. He'd only heard of this chance occurrence of moonlight and rain, but he'd never seen it before. The local *kupuna* (older people) called this colored rain *'ulalena*. They say the only place it falls in all the world is on the islands of Maui, Molokai, Lana'i, and Kaho'olawe.

Ole felt like a redeemed Phantom of the Opera or a Tambourine Man, so he turned slowly in a pirouette on one foot and sang out with his own music of the night, "I'll dance beneath the starry sky...patiently by the sea...and perhaps someday, love again will come to me."

The gentle surf anointed his feet with warm waves. The colors in the rain re-baptized him. Ole became a *Malama Nui,* a Great Light. His spirit burned like a sudden Pentecostal, illegal beach fire. He would leave no mess, only friendships on Maui. He waved one hand above his head as he danced there in his lonely life, his confident soul reaching for the distant stars.

Snorkeling with Sailbad the Sinner

Oliver Gold

Uncle Ole was on the beach at seven. The morning sun was an hour away from burning through the jungle. If you've been to Honolua Beach, you'll remember that it's not a beach at all. There is just one tiny spot of sand the size of a yoga mat that's surrounded by football-size rocks in all directions. Ole was all alone, practicing stillness in a full lotus. His mind had left his body and was linking up on the telepathic 4G Coconut Wireless that yogis, dolphins, and other sentient beings share.

Hello, friends. I'm here. You know the place. Tune in on my vibe and find me again.

There was no immediate answer, but that was

normal. When the dolphins do reply, which isn't too often, your whole brain buzzes and vibrates like a cell phone.

Uncle opened the eyes in his human form down there on the mat and searched out across the bay. Not a fin, not a splash disturbed the postcard stillness of the scene. It was, however, a crystal clear day for snorkeling.

The shallow water was a much different story. It was dirt-brown from a fresh stream that was bleeding red mud into the quiet bay. It had rained crazy hard last night. It looked like Ole was going to be sloshing through soup for the first fifty feet of his swim, not too inviting.

Ole snapped back into his body. There was still no one around. He had the whole marine sanctuary to himself. He whispered a prayer of thanks out across the still waters of the muddy bay. He grabbed his flippers and stepped barefoot, over the mossy boulders that lined the shore. With his mask on tight, he crouched in the murk and pushed one foot at a time into his professional fins. He rolled chest down onto the brown surface and with powerful kicks and long sweeps of his arms, propelled himself across the chocolate milk. When he'd swum far enough from shore, the bay turned into Fantasia, clear as a clean aquarium. There were fish everywhere, big, small fry, fat and skinny. He listened for their vibes on his telepathic sensor thing, somewhere in the middle of his forehead; it's hard to explain. The fish sounded like a hive of bees, all buzzing softly on the same frequency, but he did catch a few wild shouts:

Where's Nemo?

Gone again! We gotta find him!

Whaz up, Ono, brah?

Don't slang me with that pidgin talk, mister. If you want to stay in this school, you'll speak Ahi like the rest of your classmates.

And he heard some singing,

Under da sea, unda da sea...

Ole was swimming in less than a fathom of water; more like three or four feet. That's a little too shallow for crossing a reef of sharp coral, and as the waves lifted and dropped him, he sucked in his belly fat to avoid painful skid marks.

There were lots of what were they called? Maybe Tang? Yah, Yellow Tang, that's it. They were giving him a royal escort, swimming along next to his shoulders. Fish names, like people names eluded him, unless they were female, cute, and single.

He sent them a friendly vibe: *Hi, girls.*

Yer on another date with fish, brah. The Yang-

Tang half of his brain was so right; he should find a girlfriend.

Dude, you find 'em but you can't catch one. The Yin half was a bit sarcastic this morning.

The bright greenish-blue fish over in deeper water was one he recognized. It was a male parrot fish nibbling on a brain coral and pooping sand. Yep, it's one of those crazy facts of life. Romantic Hawaiian and Caribbean beaches are made of piles of "all-ready-been-chewed" ground-up coral. The tiny live polyps are devoured and the rest is eliminated out the fish's gills and rear as sand.

Mom Nature, she's one funny joker, laughs both halves of his brain.

Ole was amused but not smiling. You can't smile while snorkeling or you drown. Even a happy little grin lets water surge in around your air tube's mouth piece.

The other fascinating nonfiction fact of life that he knew about parrot fish was that a handsome glittering blue-green male dominates a harem of five to ten pale-looking, brown-speckled females on his private reef Casbah. He defends his women and his territory from any and all other males. When the ruling sultan dies, the most aggressive female in the pack turns into a brightly colored blue-green male.

Yes, within twenty-four hours she, or rather he, now rules the harem she was once a part of. Mother Nature, like every other woman he'd ever met, was complicated. Ole had several gay and lesbian friends and one transgender friend. He accepted them whole-heartedly as wonderful anomalies to the male-female norms of life on planet Earth.

With only the fish buzz and his thoughts to keep him company, Ole was enjoying the Zen of snorkeling alone. At least he thought he was...until he was shocked by "claws" scratching across his bare back. He nearly peed his trunks!

Wha'zat! Brah, we're not alone out here. That was a claw from above! Can't be a fish, can't be human!

He actually thought all those words in the split instant it took to spin around ready to defend himself from some unknown sky monster. There was a blur of sharp white teeth near his shoulder and bulging white eyeballs that scared him even wilder until he saw the teeth and eyes were on the smiling face of a dog-paddling, black Labrador. Ole let out a laugh which let in the sea and he choked on salt water with great relief.

His new buddy swam with him for a while until a large catamaran tour boat motored noisily into the bay.

There goes yer private swim, brah.

And to his patient chagrin, the water was soon churning with one hundred flapping flippers.

Don' be selfish, brah. Eva'body can play 'n dis park.

The fifty swimmers did spook the black lab.

Boat barf, I'm outta here. Ole was pretty sure that's what he heard the dog vibe as he swam for shore.

The lab shook himself dry and stretched out under a coconut palm. He was still smiling and panting with his tongue hanging out.

Uncle put his mask back into the water just in time to see an octopus come up off the bottom lifting up a cloud of sand from where it had been hiding. Its body was the size of a pomelo and as it pulsed away, kicking all eight legs in unison, it changed color from sand beige to bright purple in seconds.

Aloha, Ursala, he sent a mind text her way.

There was no reply. He'd scared her, and she was in a hurry to escape.

Ole was mesmerized. This was the first real octopus that he'd ever seen that wasn't dead and wrapped in cellophane in the seafood section of Safeway. Uncle's amazement bumped up to the next level as the terrified creature pumped out a cloud of black ink to hide its escape.

So cool, brah. They really do that! He kept his mouth shut this time and swam along with a cast of thousands in the new Discovery Channel fish movie, *Uncle Ole's Neighborhood.* Sorta like Mr. Rodgers; only wetter and much cooler.

There seemed to be many more fish in the shallow water along the shoreline, and it was warmer there too. He'd gone mildly hypothermic on his last swim with the dolphins. He wanted to keep his body heat close to 98 degrees. Uncle Ole knew that snorkeling alone is never a good idea but he felt safe near the rocky shore, where he could stand up and rest if he needed to.

Yah, yer fifty-five years old, betta take it easy, grandpa, cautioned the sensible half of his brain.

Shut up, smirked the foolish half.

You shut up!

It never ceased to confuse him how he could have done well in college, earned a master's degree, and taught chemistry for almost thirty years with such a juvenile brain.

We heard that, thought both halves at once.

As he snorkeled farther along the shore the water deepened to ten and then thirty feet. Soon he was swimming next to a steep vertical wall with a collection of long skinny fish. Needle-Nose Pliers? Close enough, so many fish, so many names. The water around him changed color to a deep, cobalt blue as the bottom fell away to deeper than cobalt, way down into what looked like black nothing.

Too deep, grandpa, betta go back.

Jus' a little more out, yah?

Don' do it.

Ole kept swimming. He wasn't tired or cold and he was alert now for any indication of a dangerous current that might sweep him offshore. He'd read about surfers and people snorkeling being swept away, their bodies never found. Everyone thinks Maui is Disneyland and you can't get hurt here. Ole was not a fool, especially around the ocean. Okay, maybe he was a fool for cute, rich women but he'd sailed for years up near Seattle and knew the ocean's moods could kill.

Just a few more strokes ahead of him was the outer rock rim of the bay. The deep water was colder and pushed against him, a good direction to be pushed: back into the bay instead of over to Japan. He kicked his fins hard gaining on the current and raising his head to look around the point. To the southwest he could see the shore of Molokai. To the north he tried to imagine the distant islands of Alaska, several thousand miles away.

Where all your dolphin buddies, brah?

Fo'get 'em, gramps, we swim back now.

Neva'eva' gonna forget 'em, dude, neva.'

Ole turned back toward the beach, letting the current push him inshore. But as he zipped along the rocks he found a three-foot crack with water gushing in and out. Grabbing hold of the rocks with both hands, he poked his face mask into the opening. He was surprised to find a cup-shaped, inner bay about thirty feet across: a hidden volcanic cauldron. The clear water looked shallow enough to stand in, very calm, with a sandy bottom. There were fish of a thousand colors resting in there. Uncle waited for the next wave and body surfed in with the inflow, riding its power through the crack in the rim of rocks and found himself in the center of what he would later name, "Chip, the teacup."

Oh, that's original, dude.

He didn't care. He'd discovered a new world. Uncle lowered his fins and stood on the bottom to rest. Sand rose up around his ankles and slowly settled back down.

Whoa, explorer guy, look what Maui's been hiding.

Betta rest, grandpa, while you can.

From where he stood in the cup, Ole could not see out over the edge but he heard another snorkel boat motor into the bay. He ignored it and swam all around the inside of the teacup scattering holes in the curtains of fish. Hundreds of butterfly fish, damsels, angels, and triggerfish swarmed around him. He felt like that bubbling plastic diver guy in a home aquarium. Some of the triggerfish were the masked Humuhumunukunukuapua'a, the Hawaii state fish with the supercalifragilistic name.

When he had communed with the teacup fish long enough, Ole waited for an outgoing surge and skipped school with a dozen juvenile goatfish out the chip and back into Honolua Bay.

There were now three tour boats anchored in his once quiet sanctuary. That made at least a hundred snorkel tubes scattered across the water like colorful plastic junk. No wonder there were no dolphins here this morning. He sent a dolphin warning vibe to his friends just in case they were still on the way,

Danger cousins, no can Honolua Bay. All choke full o' apes today.

Ole swam over toward the largest of the million-dollar cattle boats. The name painted in broad strokes on the side was *Sailbad the Sinner.* Ole started to laugh. Salt water was waiting for this, and rushed into his mouth choking him. He tore off the mouth piece and mask and lifted his head into the fresh air.

There were people of all ages snorkeling and splashing all around him. Some were climbing up the swim steps and gathering at the afterdeck bar. It was lunch time. Ole climbed up with them. He helped himself to a turkey sandwich and ordered a complimentary rum and Coke. The bartender made no eye contact, as per his training, and soon Uncle was enjoying the view and the booze from a comfy boat cushion on the bow of the luxurious *Sailbad.*

The world did look better from the deck of a yacht. There was so much beauty around him he could scarcely believe it, the bay, the boats, the bikinis, the boat flags, the bikinis. He struggled to keep his eyes open, but all that swimming had worn him out. He fell asleep there on the forward sundeck.

He dreamed he was a sleek dolphin and he'd met a shy lady dolphin who was too scared to swim. She was so cute with her pink inflatable water wings tightly fastened around each pectoral fin. She had movie star sunglasses on and said her name was Lorena. She smiled shyly, and he was just swimming up to touch noses when…

Ole awoke to the sound of the boat's engines

firing up. He stretched and made his way toward the stern, just another swimsuit-clad tourist with snorkel gear. As he walked past the bar, he lifted one more cello-wrapped sandwich from the counter and pulled his mask down over his face to hide his identity. He stuffed the sandwich in his shorts pocket and stepped down on the swim step. He saw no prop wash. The engines were still idling as the crew prepared to bring up the mooring lines. Holding his mask firmly onto his face he slipped into the water and stroked a beeline for the beach.

He heard the hollering as the crew and captain yelled for him to return. Everyone aboard *Sailbad* must have been stumped, wondering why anyone would want to walk all the way back to Ka'anapali Beach from here.

Ole kicked off his fins and stepped over the large rocks on the beach. He found the black lab still smiling under the coco palm. Uncle sat down next to the dog and waved to the departing yacht. Fifty people cheerfully waved back.

"Are you hungry, you handsome ol' fish tracker?" Ole unwrapped the cellophane from the sandwich. The crinkling sound brought the dog to his feet and he wagged his tail and smiled as only a hungry black Labrador can smile.

"I love this island," whispered Uncle Ole as he scratched his new friend's ears and fed him a royal lunch.

Mahalo, bruddha, he heard the dog think, in perfect pidgin.

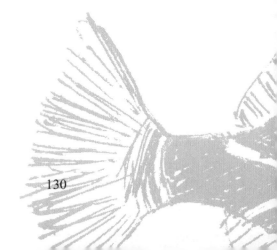

The Tremendous Difficulty of Being Good

T. A. Binkley

I am by nature not particularly philosophical. My usual tendency is to act first and to think later, but with nothing much to do as of late, I find myself wondering about love. It's one of the most important aspects of my life—the forever-after kind of love. It's long been one of my pursuits, but I'm not sure that just wanting it is enough to make it happen. My experiences since birth have made me who I am—sometimes lovable and sometimes not so much—with a bit of genetics thrown in. I've been lucky just once really—right place/right time. The person I fit with perfectly found me. We lived every day sharing new things and things we both liked doing together. We were almost inseparable.

I will admit, I'm not too good being alone. I am, however, most of the time, good at trying to meet someone else's needs, to foster what we have. But sometimes I sense my "self" getting lost along the way. My need to be loved and accepted has, on several occasions, led me to do things I ordinarily wouldn't. I remember being young, competing openly and aggressively with my brothers and sisters to get the most attention—the most love. As I grew up, the need became stronger but the way to find it less clear. I knew what it was—love. My family had loved me unconditionally before I ventured out to find it elsewhere. So, when I did find it again, I pounced on it.

Dell seemed open to my advances from the start. With her, I felt life would go on, perfectly, just as it was, forever. My heart raced. Every time I saw her, it took my breath away. I was sure that I was one of those lucky ones who finds love and is content living in the moment, without any fear of what might come next. Looking into her eyes every day, I knew we were meant to be. Even in our times of silence we were comfortable together. Watching her face told me everything she was thinking and feeling. After years of sharing and comforting each other, there wasn't much we hid from one another. I knew: *This IS the real thing. We'll be together forever. We've chosen each other. I'll never have to be alone again!*

Then, I found myself without her. She'd left me without even a real good-bye. I couldn't understand why. What had I done that was so disappointing she'd gone without a warning or even an explanation? If she'd told me she was angry or disappointed, I could have changed—tried harder for her—been better. I know I could have. Now, life was lonely—especially dinnertime. That had always been our alone time together. She'd call out, "The news is starting. Come sit with me." She'd pour a glass of red wine and we'd watch the events of the day, cuddled up side by side on the banquette. Sometimes we'd share the cheese and crackers. With the ads muted, she'd talk about working in the garden later or taking a stroll down to the river. Anticipating a walk had me jumping into her lap and licking her face before she even got up. Just the word "river" or "walk" could send me dashing for the leash.

Now there was only kibble and water in large dispensers against the kitchen wall. The dog door was always open to the fenced yard out back, but no one came or went all day. That first morning she didn't come home I ran around the lawn and rolled in the dirt hoping I'd hear her yell, "Get out of that flower bed right now! Come on, it's the river for you!" Now all the fun of running, rolling in the dirt, chasing the balls she'd throw, and dashing at the big dogs we'd encounter was gone. The rest of that day I just lay on the couch until dark, staring out the window at the driveway, waiting. When it was too dark to see, I went upstairs to bed, curling up where her feet should have been. Night after night I slept alone, waiting to hear her open the front door.

After what must have been days, a man stood in the living room. He called me by my name, Bella, and his voice and hands were gentle as he kneeled down and coaxed me to come to him. He took the leash hanging by the door and hooked me up. "Say good-bye, Bella. It's time to go—time for something new." Walking down the drive, with me dragging behind, he gently encouraged me to follow..."Good girl, Bella. It's okay."

When we reached the car, "Can you jump in or should I lift you up?" I jumped. His car smelled of dogs—lots of dogs—and greasy food. My nose was tingling from all the different smells. He drove as I stood, paws up on the sill, wondering why the window was rolled up. We stopped in front of a large cement building at the edge of town. The sign read:

ASPEN ANIMAL SHELTER

We walked in, side by side this time, and immediately I began to shake with excitement, maybe a bit of fear. The smells! There were cats (those creatures I loved to lunge at and chase), dogs, birds, and other smells I was unsure of.

Two young girls standing at the counter turned and came running over to us. "Oh, she's so cute. Can we take her for a walk? What's her name? Can we pat her?" Seth explained I was new, a little shy, and very dirty. They could come back another day to take me out. He led me behind the desk in the entryway where he sat answering phone calls and checking in dogs for vacation stays while their owners were out of town. I waited, tied up, as he led the new arrivals to the boarders' yard.

Each time he returned he'd reach down to pat my head, "It's okay. You'll be okay, Bella." As the day became quieter he took me to a small room and carefully ran his hands up and down my body pulling out debris. "Boy, you're filthy, little one. Let's get you upstairs for a bath." He took off my collar and tags and handed me to a tall young boy. Although my terrier hair was wiry short it was matted with mud and burrs from Dell's yard. I squirmed with excitement under the warm water and then again as the brush ran through my clean fur. I rolled over, feet in the air, tangled in a towel, asking to get my tummy scratched, but he didn't do it the way Dell did. I started to miss her all over again just as Seth returned and pronounced me healthy and "adoptable."

He took me to join a pack of other dogs in an open dirt yard out back. I ran in circles the minute I was put down. Being surrounded by so many other dogs was a bit frightening for someone my size, weighing in at barely twenty pounds, but I never let my trepidation show. Everyone watched. When I was sure my performance had won their respect, I stopped. We sniffed and postured, cautiously taking each other in. A golden retriever, gently carrying a stuffed hedgehog in her mouth, stepped closer to welcome me. She dropped the animal right at my feet, wagged her tail and glanced down into my eyes, looking just a little sad. Rather than feel sad myself, I dashed away again, then slowed and stopped when no one followed. I'd been thinking about something since I'd heard it. "What does the word 'adoptable' mean?" I asked.

A very handsome black lab came forward

authoritatively. "All of us in this pen," he stood tall and looked around slowly, "we're adoptable." He paused for effect. "Some of us are older, been here for years, like Jute over there," he gazed slowly to the left, over to the shaded area of the yard. "Ever heard of a sled dog?" He didn't wait for an answer. "Jute was a sled dog from right down the road. Seth saved her when he learned what they did to dogs who couldn't keep up anymore running in harness with the younger ones." He shook his head in disgust. Jute seemed to know she was being singled out. She raised her head and nodded before resting her chin back on her outstretched paws. Everyone began milling about, once again in silence.

After a bit, another dog hobbled up to me, a British cattle dog mix—brown, black and white. He raised a front leg showing off a good-sized cast, explaining sheepishly, "Bad landing. I'll do anything to keep from being left alone. This last time I tore out a screen, broke a window, and jumped from the second story. I've done it before. I destroy things to get out—can't be alone, really can't. Makes me go crazy. It's sort of like I short-circuit." He paused as if in thought. "Maybe here is best for me. I'm never alone here." He looked down and sighed. Then he went on, "I imagine there aren't many of us who'd forgo a family for this bunch, as nice as being with all you guys is, but I think I would." He stood for a bit, then continued. "See those two next door?" Houdini hopped slowly towards the fence, "Pit bulls. They can't get along with anyone but each other. I hurt myself sometimes, but those two...," he trailed off.

Jute raised her head and added, "No one ever gets turned away from here, no one. We can all stay as long as it takes to find another home or even if we don't." The black lab stood tall. "I came from a family that loved me, lots of us did, you see. We weren't really bad or anything. Sometimes who we are is hard for others to understand and accept, or things just don't work out."

I really wanted to say out loud to all of them, *I didn't get left. She didn't give up on me! She loved me. I'm not one of those dogs that someone gives up on.* But instead, I stood in silence, thinking over what they'd all said.

Another terrier mix approached quietly, "My family left me here. They moved. The new apartment didn't allow pets is what they said."

Everyone turned to the golden who once again had the stuffed toy. Her head dropped, she let go of the toy and said sadly, "There was a new baby coming soon. They decided I was too big and the house was too small." She turned away, leaving the stuffed hedgehog in the dirt. I picked it up and took it to her in the shade where she'd curled up next to Jute. Everyone was silent again, probably reflecting, as I was, on how unfair things could be.

That night, curled up with the golden and Jute in the indoor enclosure, I dreamt of Dell—her soft blanket, my head on the pillow next to hers or lying just behind her bent knees, dinner in the kitchen, and the cat next door wandering unsuspecting into the yard. I was chasing that cat and gaining.

Jute stirred and lifted her head. She saw Bella's legs churning and heard her short soft barks. Jute's lips curled in a smile and she closed her eyes to visions of racing across the ice in the Alaskan Iditarod years ago, part of a team of champions from Krabloonik, running in unison, sleeping in snow drifts under the stars or in blinding blizzards. She missed those days, but here was good too. She smiled again, this time in her sleep, content to be where she was.

Every day people came to walk us, to clean the yards or, in some cases, to adopt. It was raining the morning Jamie arrived with her two small children. I'd been watching this process for weeks now, trying to decide if I liked the people who came looking. The first thought I had that day was, *They look nice—not too clean. I could have fun with them! Kids like to play. Yeah, I want this family to be my family.* So I looked my best—attentive, smiling, bright eyed, tail held high and wagging in anticipation. They were looking at every dog that had been brought into the room, but the little girl was watching me. As soon as we made eye contact she ran over and sat down to pat me.

I climbed into her lap (careful to lick her hands and arms and not her face). I'd watched what could happen if you kissed them on the face. The moms came to the rescue with: "That one is too excitable. Wow, look at this little guy over here." My own mom had used similar distraction techniques on me and my littermates when we were all headed for a quick get-away out the garage door.

OK, I've got this. Mom is looking this way—stay calm, sit, wag a little and smile. Oh no! The little boy is headed for the cat area. Pick up a stuffed animal. Take it over and drop it by the door to those cats. Look sad. I'm better than a cat—more fun. It'll be hard if there's a cat too, but I can handle that. Pick me! Please pick me!

And so, they had. Once they were sure I was the chosen one, I got new tags on my old collar, a bag of dog food, and a new home. Now I lived in a house they called an "Aspen Tear-down." It was a long bunch of small rooms strung together, paint peeling and yard ill kept. Here, Jamie, the mom, and the kids lived happily without worrying about things getting damaged. Out back, behind the house, was a split-rail fence separating the yard from an old cemetery smelling of bear, coyote and deer. Out front was a large lawn bordering a dirt cul-de-sac with other old houses and a lot of big dogs wandering about.

I was encouraged to play in my own yard where I was supposed to be, but something kept tempting me to look for more excitement. *I'm getting restless. I need a cat to chase or something to intimidate— maybe a ground squirrel or a chipmunk. I could dig a hole or run a few circles around the yard or...* I started with the chipmunks but they were uncatchable—the woodpile they ducked into was impenetrable. *What next? Ah, here come the kids...how about a game of "catch me" with them chasing?*

I started running until they followed, then I turned and chased them. *This is great! I'm really good at chasing, but how about a little something else...I could grab hold of one of them. That would really be fun.* I jumped up and just caught the back of the little girl's sweater in my teeth. She screamed, spun around and tried to hit me, but I held on. The sweater was buttoned tight so there was no way she was getting loose. We circled until she fell, and I pounced and growled. She cried. Jamie came running and picked her up.

"Bella, no! You scared her. No more!"

I was put in the backyard to return to chipmunks and roving red ants. *But that game was fun—much better than any wild animal chase or even running with the dogs at the shelter. This makes me feel wonderful!*

The very next day I did it again, and again the day after. No amount of being told "No!" could keep me from this great new sport. *I am in charge, doing exactly what I want to do. I can't resist. I don't want to.*

The golden next door watched for several days from the cul de sac before saying sadly, "You better not keep doing that or you'll be sent back where you came from. Is that what you want?"

Is that what I want? I love to chase and run. I like the little girl and the boy, but they're getting all the attention. I only get noticed when I'm doing something they don't want me to do. No one curls up to nap with me in the afternoon or pats me when I trail after them. I sleep alone in my basket on the floor. The food's okay, but no one eats with me or takes me to the river after dinner. I'm still lonely. In the beginning, when I first arrived, everyone talked to me, wanted to walk me and hold me. They fought over who would feed me and where my basket should be at night. Now they don't. They seem to forget I'm even here. Jamie still feeds me, but she's gone all day and so are the kids. Sometimes I never even leave the backyard.

One night Jamie sat down in the kitchen with the kids after dinner. I was under the table, forgotten as usual. "Do you kids like Bella?" The little girl cried and said she had liked me at first, but was afraid of me now. The little boy said he wanted a cat.

"I don't think we're ready to have a dog. It isn't fair to her if you ignore her or are afraid to play with her," Jamie pointed out to them. The kids didn't protest as they wandered off to play. Jamie sat alone at the table, her head in her hands. She looked down and, seeing me at her feet, reached to pick me up. "Bella, our little Bella. You need a better family." Jamie put up a notice on the pet store bulletin board the very next day:

Small terrier mix, Bernese markings,
looking for a new home. Needs love and attention.
Good with other dogs—cats, not so much.
Playful, energetic and very cute.

She pinned up a picture of me, hindquarters in the air, begging to be chased. No one called. I kept making the little girl cry. Then late one Friday the phone rang, but no one picked up. I was on my own and heard the message: "I saw your ad at the pet store. I'm looking for a companion for my German Shepherd, not too big size-wise but with a big personality—a dog that can hold her own with another big personality. We're on the road a lot but have a farm in Nashville. Call...some long number. We're leaving here early tomorrow, room 303 at the Jerome Hotel."

Next morning Jamie noticed the message light blinking. She listened, then called the cell number but got no answer. She called the Jerome and asked for room 303. The operator said they'd checked out but thought they were still around back in a big silver touring bus. Jamie grabbed my leash, and we drove—fast.

There was a bus behind the hotel. The minute Jamie opened the car door I jumped out. Standing on the grass next to the bus was a big dog, a shepherd. He turned to look at me and started to trot in my direction. I stood my ground. *This is it! I know what I need to do.* I leapt in the air and ran circles around him before sitting down and looking him in the eye.

He stared back and lowered his head between his paws, butt in the air, and barked, just once. The chase was on. We circled—me chasing him, and then him me.

A young woman's voice startled Jamie. "Well, I think you've met your match, Shasta. Hi there, I'm Tanya." Jamie looked up to see a beautiful young woman in a buckskin skirt and tall boots standing on the stairs of the bus, hand outstretched.

Jamie, still stunned by this woman's appearance, put out her hand, "Jamie." Tanya was just as beautiful in person as she'd been on the *Country Music Awards* broadcast the year before. The two of them watched in silence as Bella and Shasta romped and played. When the dogs began to tire, Shasta headed for the bus steps. Bella hesitated for just a moment, then bounded up the stairs and passed right by him.

As the bus pulled out for the Country Jam concert in Grand Junction, two panting heads were hanging out the window, both smiling, faces to the wind. Tanya stood over them and shouted, "the match is made! Couldn't be better." She waved and disappeared back into the bus.

I never looked back even once. *I could finally be me! Shasta liked me just the way I was.*

Almost a year later Jamie got a call from a man

at a rest stop in Tennessee. "Did you lose a dog, cute little thing, says Bella on her tags?"

Jamie answered, "Take a look around. See a touring bus?"

"Sure do," he said.

Jamie laughed to herself, "That's her family now and thanks for helping her get back home…"

Frances

T. A. Binkley

The days were long and hot, the nights pitch black and frigid the farther north they traveled. Game had become scarce and their stores of flour, sugar and jerky were running low.

During the day, looking across endless plains, they could see to the horizon. The wavering heat waves played tricks as foothills suddenly appeared and just as quickly disappeared.

Nights brought relief from the heat, but when darkness surrounded them it was somewhat frightening. Families huddled in tents or under their wagons, listening to the cattle lowing softly as they moved about restlessly in search of water or food. The howling of coyote or wolves hunting in packs pierced the night air, inspiring the few skinny dogs still remaining to mournfully join in. The travelers had started keeping the wagons circled with the livestock in the center after spotting an Indian hunting party several days ago. Night guards carrying long guns stood watch, walking the outer rim of the circled Conestogas accompanied by bony dogs looking for unsuspecting mice or ground squirrels.

They were three months into the trip—a bit over halfway. Monotonous sun-drenched hours passed in silence with just the sound of wagon wheels turning on dirt and rock, punctuated by occasional snorts from the oxen, the crying of a baby, the whining of a child, or a mother singing a lullaby as she rocked her little one.

When they'd left Council Bluffs, the air had been electric with possibility, the excitement contagious. Everyone had been curious about their fellow travelers—why had they left their former lives behind? What visions had they conjured for a new and better life ahead? No one thought about the one person in ten who would succumb to injury or disease, dehydration or malnutrition—the ones who would never see the ocean that lay ahead.

Most had yet to see a body of water larger than a lake, but had heard stories of a vast sea filled with giant fish and sailing boats that traveled the globe to exotic ports. They'd sat in the town hall listening to stories of rich farmland waiting to be tamed and planted. Trappers told tales of abundant hunting; wild deer, bear and herds of buffalo roaming free. These stories inspired pioneers to risk their lives in the hope of new freedom, owning their own land or accumulating wealth beyond comprehension. Thousands made the long trip every year starting from Iowa or Missouri.

This wagon train had begun in May from Council Bluffs, Iowa, on the Mormon Trail, hoping to reach Portland on the Oregon Trail before winter, if all went well. They'd left later than planned, with fewer men than hoped for, and more wagons than originally envisioned. Their scout was part Indian and their pilot a young but experienced man, originally from Maine. This was his fourth trip over the Emigrant Trails and, he hoped, his last. A wife and soon a baby were waiting for him in Oregon Territory.

Frances traveled with a family from Iowa—a mother, father and three children. They'd offered her a spot in their wagon if she'd mind the three-

and five-year-old girls so the mother could care for the newborn baby boy. Frances was seventeen years old, five-foot-seven, thin, ivory skinned, with long, curly black hair braided and circled around her head, then covered with a scarf. She rarely spoke to anyone but the girls and worked tirelessly so as never to be a burden. She had with her the two dresses her mother had made, an apron she'd sewn, a pair of boots, leather moccasins, writing slates, chalk, a book of short stories and her wooden doll box.* The box, made by her father, was for her doll Clara, a gift from her parents long ago. The doll was carefully wrapped in cotton and gingham to protect her porcelain head, hands and feet from the very rough wagon ride. Even if Frances had owned more, there wouldn't have been room in the heavily laden wagon lurching over hardened ruts.

Daily, Frances sensed how far behind Owatonna really was and she knew she would most likely never return to Minnesota. The future was all she had now. The memories she treasured she also tried to keep at bay, not wanting to think about never seeing her family again.

Each day began well before daylight with a breakfast of barley mash and molasses, dried apples, and coffee—a valuable commodity that was quickly

---

*This doll box now sits in the room of the author, Frances' great-granddaughter, as a reminder of her extraordinary predecessors.

disappearing from the large canister stored in the center of the wagon. Hidden near the canister was a lockbox holding family treasures that couldn't be left behind.

Frances helped dress the girls, brushing hair and washing dirty faces and hands with a damp rag. Soon bathing would become impossible as the streams dried up and no rain was expected at this time of year. At dawn, just after breakfast, Frances helped hitch the oxen to the yoke and then she and the girls began walking beside the wagon, holding hands as they tired. Midday the travelers stopped briefly for a small meal and to rest the animals as well as their own weary legs.

Each afternoon Frances gazed mindlessly in front of her own plodding feet, kicking up dust while trying to plan a lesson in her head for the girls. Some evenings after dinner she read to them. Other nights they read to her from her one book of short stories. She'd learned long ago that studying numbers was practical and relevant and she shared this with her young charges. They kept track of the days since leaving Council City with scratch marks on the side of the wagon box and guessed at the number of miles traveled and those still to come. They tracked the moon's waxing and waning each night by sketching it on a page in her notebook and then calculating in percentages how full it was. The slate boards were used for writing numbers and letters when the ground was too hard to mark.

Frances had loved being in school. Her parents had taken great pride in her ability to excel at her studies and were overjoyed when she was picked to assist in teaching the younger children, including her own brothers, in the small schoolhouse.

Her father had said, smiling down at her as he ruffled her curls, "You'll make a fine teacher someday, little one. I never went to school myself, but you kids will."

He had a very special relationship with Frances, one he didn't share with his boys. They talked about her love of books and learning. He taught her about the earth's minerals, some of which he mined, and they kept an herb garden for home remedies. He explained to her what each plant was good for and how to dry it. Then they'd carefully label the herbs and store them in a dark dry place.

Up early each morning they shared bread and honey with the boys and her mother before he'd gather his water and food into a rucksack and head off to the mines outside town. Frances often snuck a note or a small piece of beef jerky into his pack to surprise him and then put the same treat into her own bag. When she graduated from school, she was just 16 years old. Her parents stood in the audience with pride as she received her diploma. They celebrated back home with cake and cider, and she clapped with joy when she was given her first book to keep: a collection of short stories wrapped in fine paper and tied with a big red ribbon. The tales were written by Walt Whitman, Henry David Thoreau and Ralph Waldo Emerson, among others. She'd vowed never to forget that day and the happiness that surrounded them.

Not long after, her father died in a mining tunnel collapse. Her mother, her brothers and she were left to survive on the little savings they had and the washing they could bring in from single miners in the area. Within a year her mother had remarried a man whose wife had died in childbirth along with their baby. He had two boys a bit older than Frances and was a rancher on a small farm outside of town.

From the start he perceived her as a burden, not an asset. All four boys were old enough to work the fields, but there wasn't enough washing and mending for her mother to do, let alone for Frances. The small schoolhouse could pay for only one teacher, and the longtime schoolmistress was well liked and had no plans of relinquishing her position.

When a notice was posted in the church, seeking teachers to travel to Oregon Country and the Pacific Northwest, Frances knew this might be the only way to take care of herself. She saw the sadness in her mother's eyes at night when she was helping with the dishes and then again as they sat mending and darning. The laughter and joking she'd grown accustomed to when her father was still alive was missing now. One night Frances asked, "Do you miss Papa? I think about him every day."

Tears streaked down her mother's face as she answered, "I will always love your father. For me there can never be another man like your father–but we have to go on. A mother does what she must to feed her children and keep a roof over their heads. Someday you'll understand."

Frances didn't hate her stepfather, but hated that her mother had married someone she didn't love. Her brothers didn't seem to notice the sadness and they liked working the fields. In fact, they used the farm as an excuse to cut school.

One day their mother took Frances aside in the herb garden, just coming back to life after a cold winter. "There's so little work and you know the harvest was poor last year. There's no way for me to insist that my husband support you, along with the boys, if you could do better by leaving or marrying." Frances reached for her hand and nodded sadly. Her mother was right, and Frances had no desire to marry anyone she knew.

She loved the challenge of inspiring children to learn and so she started to plan for her trip west in the hope of teaching there. Her stepfather had to travel to Sioux City the next month to buy seed before spring planting. From there she could go down river to Omaha and Council Bluffs where the wagoneers prepared for the 2,000-mile trek west. From Iowa they'd travel a short distance before several trails converged in the flatlands of central Nebraska. They'd follow the rivers and cross the Continental Divide at South Pass before heading north to Oregon Country. The northern trail ended in Oregon City, the capital of the Oregon Territory, on the Willamette River.

She read and listened, learning as much as she could about the route they'd travel, the hardships they might encounter, and what lay ahead once they reached the coast. She wrote letters to the church in Council Bluffs and heard back that there was a family named Boatwright going west, looking for help with young children in exchange for free passage. She wrote back accepting the position.

The good-byes with her mother and brothers were tearful, but she managed to sit tall and smile as she waved from the wagon box, sitting next to her stepfather in the early morning light. "I'll miss you all. I'll never forget any of you...ever," she called back.

Little was said between stepfather and daughter on the long trip to Sioux City. He was a quiet man, a good man, but serious and a bit intimidating. He paid for her river passage and she boarded the boat without looking back. She knew he'd already be gone. This was, she realized, the first time she'd been on her own, and the mix of anticipation and reservation was something new to her.

Disembarking in Council Bluffs, she found the staging area for travelers near the town's edge. It was a mix of wagons, carts, oxen, cattle, horses, families and young men looking for adventure and opportunity. Finding the Boatwright family she'd arranged to travel with was slow going with so many people and so much confusion. Dodging riders and wagons, dust rising everywhere, clutching her small bag and her doll box, she felt both exhilarated and intimidated. Men and women bustled about packing the wagons with the last of their supplies and bidding farewell to family members they might never see again, just as she'd done weeks before. Children chased each other between the wagons with dogs eagerly joining in.

The Boatwrights' wagon was being loaded with food stores that would keep over the months to come, necessities to repair the wagon's spare tack for the oxen, and personal treasures to keep something familiar close at hand. She watched Mr. Boatwright, tall and dark, strapping barrels to the side of the wagon, working alongside his wife, Ella, the two not exchanging words. They seemed to be a quiet family, reminding her a bit of her stepfather. She walked towards them. "Hello. I'm Frances, Frances Bower. Thank you for allowing me to join you." She put down her bag and extended a hand.

"Welcome," Mr. Boatwright said formally, extending his hand after rubbing it quickly on his pant leg. With handshakes and introductions all around she relaxed a bit, even smiled. The two young girls were shy, addressing her as Miss Frances and giggling before running off. She settled her things in the open wagon and set up her bedroll in the tent with the girls'. Each new dawn there was the hope that soon they would be getting underway.

Three days later, after filling water barrels and

securing the last of the fresh supplies, they left Council Bluffs. There was little time for the nostalgia she'd been working to keep at bay. Challenges arose that needed to be dealt with and a routine with duties and expectations for each girl became the solution to better discipline and to warding off the misgivings that arose. Trying to get the cattle on leads to follow the wagon proved too difficult, so they were set free to follow on their own. Getting the oxen into harness and then controlling them proved more challenging than imagined, at first requiring three people to get the work done. Frances had a lot to learn.

On the fourth morning out, the oxen yet to be tackled, she thought she heard crying coming from one of the bedrolls in the tent. The girls had been up for hours and were out visiting neighboring children, so she knew it wasn't one of them.

When she searched, she found a thin calico kitten, hiding in among the blankets. She gently put it in her apron pocket while continuing to roll the blankets and stow them in the wagon. Thinking back, she remembered the girls searching the tent after breakfast and now she knew what they'd been looking for.

As Frances yoked the oxen, she saw the girls returning, but had no opportunity to let them know she had the kitten without also alerting their father, who, she was fairly sure, had no idea there was a stowaway. The girls' secret was safe for now and in the coming weeks, the appearance of the kitten would elicit a frown but no harsh words from Mr. Boatwright. This small creature was to bring comfort and a sense of hope to all of the family.

As the days wore on, the baby started coughing. He was fussy and feverous and soon refused to nurse. Ella became restless, quieter than usual, and slept very little—trying repeatedly to coax the baby to nurse. Frances watched the little thing become weaker each day until he no longer cried at all. One morning Ella asked Frances to watch him and the girls while she helped with gathering wood and drying buffalo meat.

Frances brewed a mix of herbs, a bit of molasses, and cow's milk in a cup and offered it to the baby by soaking a clean rag and gently putting it in his mouth, stroking his neck with the other hand. He was slow to understand sucking on the rag, but once he did, the container of milk was soon empty.

She knew she'd have to explain to Ella but wasn't sure how to begin. The two were not close, rarely talking at all, and Mr. Boatwright had made it very clear that she was to interact with the girls only. That was her job. Ella's input had not been asked for, just her expertise in teaching and minding the girls. The choice on how to tell them what she'd done turned out not to be hers.

"Mommy, Mommy, Ella got the baby to drink cow's milk. She really did. There was this powder and the cow's milk, and he sucked it off this rag. See. Look. The cup is empty." Ella took the baby from Frances and started to cry.

"I don't know what you did. I don't care how you did it. I'd...I'd given up hope. Thank you." Frances smiled and led the girls off to get ready for bed.

The Boatwrights were lucky; they'd lose no one to fever, snakebite, or the accidental discharge of a rifle poorly handled. Their wagon wheels would break spokes, but infrequently, and each time they were able to make repairs and rejoin the other wagons by nightfall. The Indian sightings were always at a distance and appeared to be hunting parties, not war parties.

The days following the herbal remedy brought about a change in the women's relationship. One night Ella sat fireside rocking the baby, looking down on his pink, healthy little face, the girls safely asleep in the tent. Her husband had just left for a gathering of the men to discuss the next day's route.

"Join me, Frances, here by the fire." Ella talked about the decision to go west, a decision she had not been a part of. "I wanted to stay where we were. My whole family was there. The baby was new. The trip would be long. But the choice was my husband's."

She went on to tell Frances that she hadn't dared to object. Her duty as a wife was to follow her husband and care for the children. What she wanted she had to put aside, as a good wife and mother. Frances listened but was not sure she understood why being a wife meant giving up your own voice, your own dreams. She asked if Ella was sorry now that she'd gotten married, if she would have done it had she known they'd go west?

Her answer was swift, "No, I could never be sorry. I couldn't imagine my life without my babies. I wanted to be a wife and mother, just not out here. But we're almost there now. We're all alive and we'll have a farm and a home, and the crops will be better than they've ever been." Frances reached to stroke the baby's golden curls and let her hand brush Ella's shoulder before turning to the wagon to fetch her bedroll.

When at last the lights of Oregon City twinkled on the horizon, the end of the journey was near. That night the settlers gathered around campfires, quietly talking. A young woman with a beautiful voice started singing and soon the harmonicas came out, and a banjo joined in, followed by more voices. There was dancing and singing and storytelling. Everyone let the excitement take hold and hours later went to bed dreaming of the future, the hardships forgotten. The challenges they'd faced crossing the plains, the deserts, and the divide had once been unknown. But most people had survived. Here, again, was the unknown. Frances realized as she closed her eyes, huddled safely with the girls, that once again she would soon be on her own in a new frontier town.

After tearful good-byes with the girls, a warm hug from Ella, and a promise to write once she was settled, wherever that might be, she headed to the town hall, uncertain who might direct her to the schoolhouse. The buildings were taller than she'd imagined and the dusty streets much wider, filled with so many more people than she'd ever seen back home. She saw supply stores of grains, meat, cheeses, butter and sugar. A barber sat outside his shop watching for customers, answering questions and greeting acquaintances. A milliner's windows displayed bolts of fabric and fancy hats. The sound of laughter and organ music spilled out the open doors of drinking houses, and animated conversations escaped from hotel entryways. New arrivals headed to the surveyor's office to begin their search for good land to plant—land they could keep as their own if they farmed it. Everyone seemed to have somewhere to go.

Frances followed the directions she'd been given to the schoolhouse. It was a Saturday, and no one was about. She walked all around the whitewashed building with its peaked roof and small bell tower. She hurried up the few stairs and cautiously tried the door. As she entered, she felt warm air rush towards her and she jumped as a dove rose from the front of the room silhouetted in the bright sunlight. The air smelled of cedar planking and the wild roses she'd seen outside by the steps. "This feels right," she said softly to herself. "This is where I belong now." She breathed a sigh of relief, sure at last her decision to go west had been the right one.

She sat at a desk in the farthest corner from the door, resting her head on her arms, just for a minute, and fell into a deep peaceful sleep. She dreamt of the whip-poor-wills calling out, hunting for insects in the waning light; of her father, sitting on their porch, smoking the pipe he'd carefully packed with cherry tobacco after tapping out the last from the night before; and of her mother calling from inside, letting them know the apple pie was hot from the oven.

Suddenly she started upright, wakened by church bells. She'd slept all night. Forgetting where she was, she toppled out of the chair. *Church! I must go to church. There I might find a place to stay or a position at a nearby school....or food...yes, food.* Her stomach growled as she imagined the smell of that apple pie along with the other Sunday smells of baking bread and frying chicken.

Quickly washing her face and hands at the pump outside the door and drinking from cupped fingers she hurried towards the bell tower visible from where she stood. Smiling with joy, refreshed from her travels, and minus her doubts, she found herself skipping along as she had years earlier on her way to school.

Raised Protestant, she wondered if this church welcomed all religions, or not, but she found the doors open wide and the congregation singing a hymn she knew. Sitting in the last pew gave her a view of those in front and she saw that most, like herself, were a bit dusty, and probably, she imagined, wearing the best they had. Her head was covered with her scarf, but she noted many of the women wore hats—some very fine hats sat perched on shining hair piled high on the well-dressed women near the front.

When services were over, she waited until the crowd thinned before approaching the minister. From his long robes she knew he was a Methodist, young and stocky with a grin that hadn't left his face since she'd begun to watch him conversing with his flock. He turned in her direction just as she came close and was about to speak. "Hello there. I'm Pastor Dan, and you are?"

Frances blushed and stumbled on her own name, "Frances, Frances Bower." She flattened the front of her skirt self-consciously. He offered his hand as she struggled with how to begin. His silence, while still holding her hand, calmed her as she stood taller, "You see, I've come by wagon, from Owatonna, in Minnesota, just yesterday. The newspapers and flyers posted there, in our church, said teachers were needed out west. I'm a teacher," she paused. "I thought perhaps you would know if there are any positions here...in Oregon City."

She waited as he looked her in the eyes and smiled, "You may just be in luck, young lady. There just might be. The schoolmistress has a new baby, her first child, and needs help with the teaching to allow for more time to care for her daughter. Let's walk that way, shall we?"

Frances impressed Mrs. Dumont over coffee

and sandwiches and so she not only began to assist the following Monday, but also was offered a room to let.

This teacher loved the children in much the same way Frances did, marveling at their curiosity and desire to know more. School kept the children from having to work in the fields most every day, and this may have encouraged their participation.

Soon Frances was doing more than just handing out materials and correcting lessons. As her confidence and expertise increased she needed more of a challenge—a classroom of her own. Frances was ready when Mrs. Dumont said, "It's time. You're ready to do this on your own. Let's see where there might be a position for you."

The following Sunday, five months after Frances' arrival, Mrs. Dumont's younger sister came to live with her and her husband. Frances needed to move on, but where? Pastor Dan had a colleague who lived outside of Spokane Falls, Washington, a new fast-growing settlement on a river, with land rich with resources. The newcomers wanted a school and a church and a township where now there were hunters, trappers, lumbermen, Indians and the few settlers. The prospect of traveling 250 miles was far less daunting after the previous 2000-mile trip, and the idea of her own classroom was exhilarating. As soon as the winter thaw allowed, Frances joined a group of supply wagons headed for Davenport and then on to Fort Spokane just north.

Her arrival had been eagerly anticipated by the minister, Homer, and his wife, Evelyn. She was invited to stay with them in their small cabin. Evelyn was young, about her age, and Frances sensed that another woman's presence might be comforting. "We can pick blackberries and make pies. I'll show you how to quilt. It will be so much fun!" Evelyn said with excitement that first night at dinner.

The church was under construction next door. The women brewed coffee, squeezed lemons for lemonade, and baked cookies for the men toiling in the sun or the rain. Evenings they sat measuring material for the church curtains, cutting the fabric carefully, and sewing long panels together for the windows. They stuffed cushions for the pews putting Frances' sewing skills to good use. Homer noted that the two women were more like sisters than just friends.

Homer assured them that once the church was complete, the school would be built next, but Frances could begin teaching in the home of a lumberman, a close friend of his, who was rarely in town. John was a church-going man and had only lately begun traveling for his business.

"John Kendall's dream is to build the first sawmill and forge on the river—to supply the entire area with construction lumber, building supplies, metal fittings and fasteners. He has investors and needs suppliers and skilled workers to make that dream come true."

The schoolhouse and a small cottage next door were clearly Frances' dream, but until its completion she'd accept the kind offer of the lumberman. The large well-built house with its shuttered windows and wraparound porch would do very nicely. She wrote a letter to thank Mr. Kendall for his offer and sent it to his solicitors to forward on. She would start teaching just after the spring planting.

Frances' pupils ranged in age from six to sixteen with many having never attended school but rather having studied whatever their parents, of their own free will, could teach them at home. Few children were sitting in this large, open, paneled room off the kitchen. The older boys looked at Frances with more interest in her figure than in the figures she hoped to introduce. But it wasn't long before she'd won their respect. She could play a mean kickball, sew a torn pant leg to avoid a scolding from home, bake cookies when they paid attention well, and tell tales of her adventures crossing the plains, deserts and mountains.

Everyone she met seemed to want her to come round for supper. She was introduced to brothers and uncles, and no one was hesitant to assist her in finding a husband. Frances wasn't sure she appreciated their efforts. The idea of marriage had never held appeal after losing her father and seeing her mother marry a man she barely knew in order to survive. Hearing firsthand about wifely duties from Ella had only reinforced Frances' doubts about the institution of marriage. She quite comfortably explained, "I'm really so busy with the children. I love them all so much that I really think of them as my family now. There's much to be done what with the church and the new school being built and lessons to plan. But thank you for your concern, really."

Only Evelyn was close enough to ask her, "Do you really not want to get married? Ever? That's all I wanted—to get married and have children. Homer's ready now, for children, I mean. Are you sure there's no one that you fancy?" Frances loved Evelyn like a sister, one she'd never had, but their lives were different. She saw how happy Evelyn was but wondered in silence if there were many men as loving and supportive as her father or Homer. She had a feeling that if the man she was to marry were among all the suitors she'd been introduced to, she'd have known it.

Summer passed slowly with school closed for a month at harvest time in late August. Frances sewed drapes for the large room she'd transformed into a classroom, hoping to ward off the coming cold of winter. She stayed at the house most nights, quilting after school in front of the potbelly stove to give Evelyn and Homer more time alone. Some evenings, falling asleep in the warmth and solitude of the house was too tempting to resist, and everyone knew that's where Frances was if she didn't make it back to the cabin. Before long, Evelyn was pregnant, the church was completed and the first snows were falling.

Magically each morning a stack of wood appeared outside the kitchen door. After several weeks she noticed the older brother of two sisters attending her classes standing outside just a bit too long after all the children had filed indoors, anxious to get out of the cold and their damp coats. The young man always came early to pick up his siblings, waiting silently on the back steps until school ended. One day Frances waved as the three of them walked away hand in hand, and he smiled. The weather was getting blustery and colder. Frances was spending more time at the house rather than braving the trek back to the cabin.

One morning, as she was getting the fire started in the stove to warm the room for lessons, she heard footsteps at the kitchen door and opened it to find the young man she'd seen with his sisters bent down unloading his arms of wood. He dropped the last logs suddenly and stammered, "I didn't mean to frighten you...I...I just thought you might be cold, the weather and all. Samuel, I'm Samuel."

She waited for him to stand fully upright. "Well, Samuel, I haven't been cold at all with all this wood you've brought me. Thank you. Please, come in. I have coffee." He wiped his hands on his pants, thanked her, bowed slightly, and entered.

And so it began. Every morning he'd join her for coffee near dawn. They'd talk about weather and food and the town's progress towards being "civilized" and then he'd leave to get his sisters. He asked about her trip west, her family, and her hopes and then he told her about his family and his hopes. He wanted to learn to read and to know his numbers. "My father thinks I'm too old to learn or maybe too stupid."

Samuel told her how his sisters had tried to help him but weren't very good at it. They'd prodded him, "Ask Miss Frances. She's so nice and she won't think you're stupid or anything. She says everyone can learn whatever he or she wants to if they try. Ask her, Samuel." And so, finally, he had.

Frances was pleased, a bit surprised a nearly grown man wanted her help, but still, pleased. The lessons began over coffee each morning before classes, and he took home a reader to study on his own after chores. The wood kept coming, the winter dragged on, and Frances found herself living in the big house, not even trying any longer to return to the cabin. Samuel built her a frame and brought a mattress filled with horsehair, setting it up by the living room hearth. The children loved to take turns reading on that platform in front of a warm fire if a parent was late picking them up on those days too cold and dangerous to walk home alone. It wasn't long before Samuel was able to add, subtract, write and read *The Timberman,* the local paper, front to back. He stood tall now, no stammering, and he applied for his own homestead, farming the land right next to his father's.

Frances couldn't imagine life without Samuel's friendship but was glad he hadn't chosen to court her, yet. Most of the church folk and his own sisters assumed he would once he had proven he could stand on his own. Frances caught herself staring at his hands, cupped around his mug, while seated at the kitchen table. He only came by now on Sundays to escort her to church. She realized how comfortable she was with him. They were more than just friends, but she still didn't know if what she felt for him was enough. They were equals like her mother and father had been. They spoke easily of many things—unlike the Boatwrights, who had barely spoken to each other at all. He had his own dreams and was slowly building his worth, planting feed and raising pigs for slaughter. As his eyes met hers, he reached for her empty mug and they both smiled. He stood and took it to the stove to top off.

The ground soon began to thaw and the birds slowly reappeared. Frances imagined they migrated north from somewhere south of Spokane. She'd never seen or heard a whip-poor-will out west but still dreamed of their call and the smell of her father's cherry tobacco. In her dreams her father was young and her mother stood smiling in the crook of his arm. Her brothers fought over second servings of apple pie, and she teased them about their inability to act respectfully towards each other.

Her thoughts wove their way around her family until slowly she was aware of the smell of coffee. It roused her from her reveries. As she rolled over on the mattress, she opened her eyes. She was staring up in to the face of a stranger. Pulling the quilt close around her neck, she opened her mouth, but nothing came out. He stepped back a bit and said, "I can see they were right when they told me you'd made yourself at home here. Not that I mind really. However, they didn't tell me how pretty you are. Coffee?" He turned, not waiting for her to find her voice, and walked towards the kitchen, adding, "I'm John by the way, John Kendall."

As he bowed his head to pass under the kitchen door frame, Frances realized how tall John Kendall was. His shoulders were broad and square, his arms long and muscular, his sleeves rolled to the elbow. Frances also thought, as she watched him walk away, that she'd never considered he would appear some day. *It was silly of me not to have thought about that—his eventual return. After all, he'd built a beautiful home presumably to occupy.*

She sat up slowly, clutching the blanket, wondering just what kind of a man he was. She could see he had a sense of humor. He was good with words and at ease in her presence. *Why is it I'm still sitting here gawking? Get up and get dressed, you silly girl. He's quite young, younger than I'd imagined.*

She hurriedly exchanged her nightshirt for a skirt and blouse, being sure she was out of his line of sight. She gathered her few things into the case stashed under the bed and quickly glanced into the mirror over the fireplace. She tucked a few loose strands of hair behind her ears.

Unsure how next to proceed she stood in the kitchen doorway watching him put out two coffee cups with matching saucers and small plates, slice the bread from the bread box, and open the lid of a jar of preserves she was sure hadn't been there earlier. He sensed her eyes on him as he moved purposefully in his own kitchen. Without actually facing her, he motioned to a chair at the kitchen table. After he saw her sit, out of the corner of his eye, he approached and poured the coffee into the cups on the table, returning the pot to the stove before sitting down opposite her. Reaching for the bread, he passed the plate to her, waiting before taking a thick slice for himself. The jam came next, and then silence as they both ate.

Frances wasn't sure what to say or do, the reality being that she'd begun to think of his house as her home, not just where she taught. *Where will I teach if he stays?...or live now that he's returned?...*

not that it's his concern, but it is mine. Evelyn and Homer will certainly take me back. Perhaps John's only here for a day or two. Where's he been all these months anyway?

Her musings were cut short by the sound of wood dropping on the kitchen stoop. John stood casually and opened the door to Samuel just as he straightened. "Mr. Kendall, you're back. I don't believe anyone expected you. You've met Miss Frances?"

"Yes, Samuel, isn't it? I have met Miss Frances, and we were just about to get to know each other. Are you a student now? I do believe you were farming with your father the last time I was here."

"Well, Mr. Kendall, I'm not exactly one of her students here but...I mean, I don't actually attend classes, but Miss Frances has taught me to read and do figures. I have my own place now, next to my father's."

"And you bring wood."

"Yes, sir. I do." The silence drew itself out before Samuel said, "Well, if there's nothing else Miss Frances…"

Frances stood and walked towards the open door. She thanked him for the wood and assured him she would see him Sunday, for church. Standing next to John, close enough to touch, as he softly closed the door, she felt oddly at ease, like the mistress of the house despite the fact it wasn't her house and she didn't know John. Seeing Samuel standing across from John she'd caught herself realizing the feelings she had for Samuel were not the same feelings she had when sitting across from John. *This a feeling I've never had before—this feeling of excitement and yet at the same time this comfort. Is this what it feels like to know you've met someone really special?*

She returned to the table. She'd read stories about love, about finding a soul mate, and wondered if this man might be just that—her soul mate. Time would tell. She'd understood the concept, but never understood how it could be so simple—seem so right. When she looked up, his eyes were on hers and with his slow smile she knew he felt the ease of it all too. It was just that simple.

The following months brought the completion of the schoolhouse and a small, attached cottage for the school mistress. Samuel continued to walk Frances to church each Sunday but he sensed a change in her. As the weeks went by he realized that Frances would not be the one he would pursue.

John was home more often now. When he was, Frances was invited to dine with him at the hotel.

He made it clear how much he enjoyed her company and consulted her often with regard to his plans for the lumberyard, listening to her suggestions on bookkeeping and hiring. She knew everyone in town far better than he did with so many recent new arrivals. In the fall, seven months after that first morning they'd sat across from each other over coffee and jam, John and Frances were married.

The church was filled to capacity to witness the union of two loved and respected townsfolk. Children in their Sunday best rolled in the grass just outside the open doors. The ceremony and reception following outdid any event this little town had ever seen, but not just in sheer number of attendees. The Kendall house, where everyone adjourned after the ceremony, was filled with food, flowers, music and dance. No one was left out when the only teacher in town and the lumberman who offered jobs to so many of the residents of Spokane joined hands.

Frances wore her first ever hat and added a veil dotted in small embroidered flowers. Her hair hung in loose ringlets framing her face. Satin gloves to her elbows covered her small hands as they clutched a bouquet of lilies, the train of her dress drifting behind her down the aisle. Evelyn stood at her side, as Frances' maid of honor, and Samuel gave her away. Samuel's fiancé smiled at them both as they walked arm in arm. She hoped soon Samuel would stand tall at the altar as John did now.

At the reception Pastor Homer toasted them both. His heartfelt respect and praise for young Frances brought tears to the eyes of many. "Frances is a very singular woman. She traveled across more than 2,000 miles of wilderness, on her own, to make her dreams come true. She's given every family—every child here today—a chance to have their dreams come true. And John. Well John, you couldn't have imagined a better partner to help you achieve your dreams. God bless you both."

Frances' mother had sent a handkerchief of homemade lace and a picture of her brothers standing tall on either side of their mother. The note read, "God bless you, Frances and John. Our hearts will be with you on your wedding day. I wish you the kind of love I shared with your father."

John and Frances had three children together, two boys and one girl. His company, the Standard Lumber Company, was the first full-service mill, lumberyard, builders' supply, forge and fuel station in the area. He had built five lumberyards in Washington and one in Idaho by the time he died. Frances and her daughter Jean took over running the business until Frances' death.

She never forgot her family in Owatonna although she never saw them again. With John gone, she'd made her daughter promise to return her to her birthplace when the time came. Jean and her daughter, Marian, did just that, accompanying the casket by train to Minnesota one colorful fall, laying Frances to rest in the family plot with her mother, father, and two brothers who had all preceded her.

Frances would have been over a hundred years old that next summer. To celebrate, her children and grandchildren opened the house once again to all the townsfolk with food, music, dance and the white lilies that Frances had carried down the aisle. This time the lilies were arranged in large vases, as striking now as they had been on that spring day more than eighty years before.

Remember Bobby

T. A. Binkley

Grace's Bobby

Dinner had been served and eaten, the dishes washed and dried, and the counters emptied and scrubbed. Grace quietly padded up the narrow winding staircase off the kitchen, past her husband's closed door and into her dressing room. She slowly changed into silk silver-gray pajamas and retrieved the latest historical novel she was already halfway through.

She loved history. When asked why, she always said, "It's all done, fact, like it or not. You know the tale comes to an end more or less based on someone's actual life—no real surprises. What matters to me is how good the storyteller is—how real he or she makes it. Some writers are accurate, offering factual details but not offering up the person. Then there are others who transport me into someone's life, spinning a sense of the real onto each page. These are my favorite writers." These are the books she'd seek out, often reading them more than once, cover to cover. Her son, Bobby, was an excellent judge of worthy works and articulate authors and he liked her to read to him late at night. It wasn't at all unusual for him to know more than the writer did about certain events or times gone by.

Grace sat with Bobby every night now, from ten to six. She was skilled at changing his position in the hospital bed, adjusting pillows and foam to ease hot spots, and holding a straw to his lips when he was thirsty. She changed the record when the needle lifted and the silence seemed begging to be interrupted. But Bobby wasn't just her patient. She wasn't just his nurse—he was her older son. Never had she imagined, when she finished nursing school so long ago, that it would be her own son she'd be caring for. Now, every evening, she cherished the time alone they shared, even as the sadness ripped at her heart. Watching a child suffer, especially your own, and knowing he will only get worse is unbearable.

She tried to shut out her sadness, especially as she entered his studio, book in hand, a smile on her face.

His illness had begun when he was 26, traveling alone in Europe. His knee had started to ache and swell, forcing him to buy a cane to take pressure off the offending limb. Returning home his doctors speculated that the overuse during travel, along with his subsequent inability to stand still when lecturing, were the contributing factors to his growing pain and swelling.

He was a professor of U.S. History at Columbia University. This class is required by most institutions, but disliked by most students. His love of the subject and his unbridled curiosity about the real stories, as opposed to the ones in history books, inspired his students to grow from a class of twenty to a class of over a thousand. Other professors teaching the same subject gladly gave it up, thus facilitating Bob's move from a small classroom to the largest venue on campus.

His reputation as a scholar and inspired orator preceded him, and he soon had friends in high places. He was offered a covert opportunity to view history in the making for President Dwight Eisenhower. His European trip on semester break was designed to assess firsthand how part of the

President's New Deal project was working, which it didn't seem to be at all. Bob reported back that all the farming machinery being sent by the United States to aid farmers in Europe was not only too large for their smaller farms but was also labeled "Gift of the USSR" before the shipping crates even left the docks.

Returning to his teaching at Columbia, he found that his knee had continued to worsen. His doctors reevaluated their overuse diagnosis to rheumatoid arthritis, an autoimmune disease not well understood, with few known options for a cure. Soon the pain and the rapid progression of the disease to other joints in his body brought him home to Selma, California, in the San Joaquin Valley and to the support his family offered. He tried cortisone and prednisone to slow the progression of the disease, but both had terrible side effects. The pain medication he found even more devastating as it dulled his thinking and rendered his memories less accessible. Nothing arrested the debilitating disease.

His cane became a crutch and then two crutches and then a walker. The walker morphed to a wheelchair and then to a reclining version of the same to allow him to rest without being lifted back to bed, a very painful maneuver. When he first accepted the use of a wheelchair, he was able to roll himself onto the large patio outside the plate glass windows making up one side of his studio. His open living space, a recent addition, was modern and bright in comparison to the rest of the old quarry stone homestead. The patio was centered around an old maple tree crawling with June bugs that sang at dusk in summer. A winding ramp at the far edge of the patio gently descended to a packed dirt drive that circled the house.

He was free to wheel himself about, stopping to gaze out at the vineyards in the distance, watching scurrying quail and bounding, lean jackrabbits. Beyond the house lay fields of plums on one side and grapes on the other. Behind the triple carport opposite his patio ramp was a large cement pool with its edges a foot above ground, grass surrounding a narrow footpath that circled the rim, dropping downhill and away from the water. Beyond, in the shade of the trees, were flowering shrubs and beds of multicolored iris.

Grace often watched him from a distance, tears in her eyes, remembering him running about the farm with his younger brother, Ted, lying in the straw with Violet while counting her newborn piglets, "accidentally" falling into the irrigation ditches, and bringing home snakes curled around his neck, face agrin. He was an exacting child, wanting to understand things below their surface, constantly reading. He loved a challenge. One year in high school he and his brother practiced hours for the upcoming talent show. They created a tap shoe routine that won them first place and went on to put together a jazz ensemble for the following year.

Bob never complained as a child and didn't as a grown man. Perhaps he too relived the same childhood memories Grace did as he wheeled around the drive, stopping to listen and watch. Now, unable to get about easily, he looked forward to rousing debates with students and friends who stopped by to visit. Sometimes the pain wouldn't allow him the pleasure of their company. But when it did, the hours raced by, and Bob forgot about his pain and his limitations. The days after were filled with Grace retrieving books from floor-to-ceiling shelving, checking facts and gathering articles from recent publications to compare new events with the old.

Then there was summer. He eagerly anticipated the arrival of his nieces and nephew as the holiday break drew near. They brought the perspective of youth back into his life as they rendered up their school stories and impressions of life in a big city.

Early each morning, before he awoke, they'd scour the fields for blue-belly lizards and pick ripe green grapes and purple plums to bring back to him. When they spoke of their days on the farm, Bob would close his eyes to better feel the joy of running carefree. He'd query, "How high are the irrigation ditches flowing? How many lizards did you catch and free? Where's the best silt now for making clay?"

They'd laugh and often sit out on the patio, the kids fashioning miniature sandwiches from oyster crackers and honey peanut butter, not eating any until the entire mixing bowl was full. These encounters with the children and with his friends freed him from his small sphere and challenged his intellect. They brought him joy, but best of all was the memory of his niece's summer reading books that she lugged into his room with a heavy heart and declared an impossible task to accomplish. He knew how to make books come alive and Grace knew it took him back to his years of teaching, a time she was sure he missed.

On bad nights, when the tears were streaming down Bob's cheeks, Grace couldn't just sit there. She'd kiss him gently and quietly open the pocket doors to the formal living room and the parlor beyond. She'd draw the velvet drapes and sit in the moonlight at the baby grand piano, playing Beethoven or Bach or Chopin. She would sing like she had in the Baptist choir; a soprano who could astound a congregation as she belted out hymns or opera arias. She was thus transported to another world that soothed her mind and helped Bobby drift off as the pain meds took hold.

Her younger son Ted's children, waking to the distant sound of her singing, huddled with sleepy eyes at the top of the front room staircase—just out of sight—and listened to the classical music. It was music they'd never heard anywhere else and would never forget.

On some nights, when their father Ted was there too, they'd hear his saxophone or clarinet weaving in and out with her voice and the piano. In this world, all was well—there was peace. All that Grace could offer Bobby now to ease his suffering was her presence, her music, and her love.

My Elder Son, Robert

I'm a doctor, not a specialist, and certainly not an expert in the field of rheumatology. I am the father of a young man, Robert. He's dying slowly in front of me and there's nothing I can do. I studied to practice medicine, was blessed to find and marry Grace,

"Billie" to her friends, and went on to establish a successful practice. With Billie at my side, nothing seemed impossible. We were married on a Friday, the day after I finished my residency at the UC Medical Center in San Francisco. The hospital where we'd both studied and worked was research based, treating patients from around the world with diseases both rare and complex. Our training, we thought, prepared us for anything we might encounter in the small farming town of Selma, California. We drove there early that Saturday and put together our second-story office in time to open on Monday.

We delivered babies, stitched up gashes, treated fevers, diagnosed disease, and offered remedies prepared in the pharmacy below.

Our two boys, Robert and Ted, sat with cherry cokes at the counter after school on weekdays, doing their homework until the last of our patients were taken care of, sometimes well after dark. No one complained.

Weekends we walked the farm, watching the harvest in fall when the migrant workers picked the grapes and laid them out on wooden flats to dry or loaded them for shipping to the winery. We treated spider bites and heat stroke, coughs and fevers. Billie brought lemonade to the pickers, and Robert read stories to the younger ones in the shade of the trees. Fall brought rain and pruning and back to school. Winter centered on the holidays, family gatherings, and gifts abundant.

The boys grew up strong and determined to strike out on their own as soon as possible. They both attended the University of California in Berkeley, as I had, and went on to follow their own dreams. Robert became a professor at Columbia, and Ted a vascular surgeon at UCSF. Billie and I stayed on at the farm and the practice. Holidays were blessed with visits from the boys and gifts brought by neighbors who'd needed our medical help but had no way to pay for it. There were chickens and walnuts, preserves and pies, and quilts and potholders. Life was full and warm and happy. Ted married, and we had three grandchildren. Bob became enthralled with politics and history, immersing himself in studying and teaching. He came home to visit after his European trip with a cane.

"Dad, they think it's rheumatoid arthritis. I've studied what I can, but there isn't much to be done."

Billie and I were left to research on our own after he left, finding, as he had, how little progress had been made since our medical school days. And then he came home to stay.

And now, I can't do what my wife Billie does. I can't spend hours at Robert's side without breaking down in tears. I've never been weak or turned away from a challenge. With my patients I control my emotions, hide my sadness, and give them the strength to face hard times. But with my own son, I can't. All I can do is get him anything that may help.

I found a physical therapist to come twice a week. He's become my boy's friend and still comes, even now, when Robert can't stand to be touched. When the bones in his neck fused, I designed an overhead mirror that allowed him to see whoever was seated at his bedside. When his toes and ankles could no longer be moved or touched—no longer able to tolerate even the weight of a bedcover—I found a metal arch to hold the sheets off his frail legs.

When Billie is getting ready to spend the night with Robert, I often retreat to paperwork in my home office. But there are some nights, after dinner, I slide open the door to the studio, dismiss the day nurse, put on a jazz record, and settle into a big leather chair near Robert's bed. I pack my pipe with cherry tobacco, light it and inhale, exhaling a stream of thick smoke. I can hear Bob let out a sigh and feel his eyes on me, looking up at the mirror overhead. I sense his smile and I know that he knows I love him beyond words.

When Billie pads in quietly, I kiss her, gently touch Bob's shoulder, and descend into the cool basement below. Uncovering the old pool table, I run my hand over the mahogany and felt, choose from the cues and rack the balls. Playing alone in the dim light transports me back to the nights of betting and winning that helped finance medical school, but I can never forget for long what's going on above me.

The studio, the mirror, the therapist—all of this is so little. All I can give Robert are the "creature comforts" that do nothing to change the outcome. What I've overcome to be a physician—the lack of support from family, the absence of funds, the move to a small farming town—can't compare with what my boy has to live with, will have to live with, from here on. My love is too great to watch death approaching…this, I leave to Billie and hope that she can understand my grief and my feelings of hopelessness and love me still.

My Uncle Bob

I'd known my Uncle Bob all my life. He was my father's older brother. He listened. No one before had really heard me or looked at me the way he did.

No one I'd ever known was twisted and crippled like he was. If he hadn't been my uncle, if I hadn't known him first with just the cane, he'd have scared me, with the electric bed, the overhead mirror, and the strained looks he struggled to hide. Sometimes I could see the fear or pity in the eyes of the people bearing books or flowers who came to visit and had difficulty keeping the conversation flowing. They came, I think, for grandma's sake and counted the minutes before they could go without seeming too hasty. They breathed out as they left the room— thankful, I ventured, that Bob wasn't their son or brother or…

I loved being on the farm. The days I liked best were when Bob's former students or school friends came round. They were a loud bunch, all talking over each other, debating the veracity of current events and questioning their impact. It seemed like arguing, unless you knew that this was their way of thinking things through and assessing different viewpoints.

Bob explained, "If we all felt the same way, there'd be no fun in it. There's never just one right side on any controversial issue. Watch and listen. Gather it all in. Then let yourself be heard." I didn't feel ready to be heard or old enough to be well-informed, but he insisted I could be.

The summer I remember best, I came to Selma angry—very angry. I didn't understand grown ups, in particular my parents. On the one hand they told me how grown-up I was. They'd given me the responsibility of watching after two younger siblings every day after school. They were always saying how proud they were of my grades. Then, instead of being honest with me, they'd let me finish out 6th grade, make plans with my friends for 7th grade, and then let it drop I wouldn't be going to the new middle school. I would instead be going to a private girls' school across town where I'd be safe, I'd get a better education, and I'd have more opportunities. They retold the story of my "aunt" June, really not my aunt at all, actually more like my godmother, who'd taught American literature in the high school nearby. She'd been knifed just walking down the hall from one classroom to another. She hadn't taught since and rarely left the house at all now. So my parents explained, "We're not taking any chances and surely you can understand that."

"But her knifing," I vehemently pointed out, "doesn't have anything to do with me. I'm not a teacher. Other kids tease me, but I really do have skinny ankles and buckteeth. All my friends are just like me—nobody wants to be around us. We're invisible most of the time. We're not worth attacking and certainly not worth going to jail over."

No change of heart was forthcoming, even after that impassioned plea. What I did get was a pile of books I had to read before school in September. *Ivanhoe?* The jacket flap said it was set in the 12th century, the time of the Crusades—a bunch of guys fighting. *Huckleberry Finn?* Something about a river. *To Kill A Mockingbird*—that one really sounded awful! I was a less-than-stellar reader and rather enjoyed someone reading to me from *Little House on the Prairie* or *Charlotte's Web*. And it wasn't at all fair to be forced to give up my friends and go to school somewhere new. I was sure that as soon as I explained all this to my Uncle Bob he'd understand and be able to plead my case more eloquently than I had.

The train ride from San Francisco, where we lived, to Fresno, near the farm, was long and hot. The dining car, however, with its white linen tablecloths, heavy flatware, gloved waiters and double-sided menu, was a wonderful distraction. Mom hoped that eating would take our minds off the heat and the scratchy train seats. She was too tired to say no when all three of us begged for banana splits and root beer floats. She'd hoped Dad would be with us on this trip south, but he'd stayed behind to perform an emergency surgery no one else wanted to even attempt. These were the ones he always was willing to risk, hoping a new technique he'd come up with or a new material he'd been testing would offer the solution. He'd called his parents to explain and arranged for granddad and grandma, "Gommie" to me, to be waiting for us at the station. Our dad had grown up very aware that his father was the only doctor in a small town and had always put the welfare of others before his own. He worked just as hard as his father did and often found himself putting his patients' needs ahead of his family's.

I sat back in the dining car, too full to move, closed my eyes, and thought about the pool—filled with freezing clear mountain runoff that had traveled in ditches from the faraway hills to fill our cement pool. Twice a month it was emptied and scrubbed by hand, bleached in the sun, and then whitewashed. All the neighbor kids stood along the edges of the rim to watch the first water rush in, and then we all slid down the slope to get to the flat narrow bottom, letting out screams as we tumbled into the icy cold water. Quickly we were all scrambling back up and out to lie shivering on the warm cement around the pool.

Uncle Bob always said he could hear us from his patio perch. I thought about what I'd overheard just before we left the city. Dad had said to Mom, "Bob's bones—his legs, back, neck—are all fused now. He can't roll out onto the patio on his own anymore. Should we tell the kids or not?" They never did, but now I knew.

The day we arrived was a particularly bad one for my uncle. He didn't want us to see him. At dinner grandpa Robert sat at the head of the table with his long graying handlebar moustache waxed and turned up perfectly. He waited until Gommie left the room before he grabbed the serving plate of jello (a ring set with green grapes on iceberg lettuce) and jiggled it into a raucous dance that split the ring. We were all laughing, the sadness of Bob's pain forgotten for the moment. Just as Gommie backed through the swinging door with the meat and potatoes, grandpa Robert quickly returned his hands to his lap in innocence. Smiling ever so slightly, she scolded us about playing with our food—that smile was just what grandpa had been hoping for.

After dinner, Gommie did as she always had. She scrubbed the kitchen counter as if the tile could go from off-white to white and ironed more sheets than we had beds. Teddy (my younger brother), leaning over into the laundry chute after we'd been sent upstairs to get ready for bed, fell headfirst from the second floor to the first. He landed on the floor of a kitchen cupboard just as the ironing board was being returned to the very same closet. The usual bedtime story was postponed until damages could be assessed. Not much laughing going on just then, but there seemed to be no serious injuries. So a story was read and we fell asleep listening to the sound of the piano chords and soft singing from the parlor. We were too tired to sneak out of bed to listen from the landing.

The next day Uncle Bob heard my tale of woe and he did "get it." We talked about protecting the people we love. We talked about good intentions and mistakes and forgiveness, about anger and disappointment. But mostly we were talking about what it meant to be a family. We drank root beer floats to give us the strength to open the first book— Ivanhoe. He told me tales of the Crusades—the battles, the triumphs, the beliefs that fueled the conflicts and the spoils due the victors. I found myself wanting to hear more. I read out loud and every time I stumbled or seemed confused, we'd stop. He told me which book to pull out and which chapter to turn to. Sometimes we listened to music or talked about things in my life that mirrored the ideas or events in the book. Some days he just sent me out to lie under the trees, pick fruit, catch lizards and return with my own stories to tell. We speculated on Ivanhoe's life—the things not said, the choices not made.

I often fell asleep thinking of the many things Uncle Bob would never get to do, so many choices he'd never get to make, and so many experiences he was now sharing with just me through our reading, our thoughts and his music. He wanted me to know how to look and really see, to decide for myself, to live strong. I realized slowly, that summer, he was giving me everything he valued in his fellow human beings because we were family and he cared.

I became aware only later how much he had made me, *me*. At school I was asked to write about the person who most influenced me when I was growing up, the one who had helped me to be who I am today. That person was my Uncle Bob. I often think back, remembering us closing our eyes, feeling the breeze from the open patio doors, smelling the ripening fruit, and hearing the doves calling in the distance. Sometimes I'd think that he'd fallen asleep until he'd say, "Isn't this wonderful! Just the two of us."

Visions

T. A. Binkley

Soccer camp was much as he'd imagined it would be. Since his camp days, very little had changed. The kids were enthusiastic about playing, but their skills were not much different than those of untamed colts let loose in an open field on a sunny day. They often tripped each other, tumbling and losing control of the ball. Watching them made him smile, remembering his own unbridled enthusiasm and his lack of skill when he'd first started to play football, or soccer, as they call it in the States.

He'd been recruited to coach in Humboldt County, California, only a week before camp started, replacing an injured veteran who was discouraged from attempting to weather two months housed in a platform tent.

So Geoff had stepped in to work with the teen girls. His tent mate, a young Aussie named Case, had also played professionally and then turned to coaching. He and Geoff hit it off immediately, neither of them ready to discuss the eventuality of spending less time on a soccer field. That first night they compared their professional and coaching experiences over beer and pretzels before turning in. Case was secretly glad that his charges were young males, unlike Geoff who was venturing into unknown coaching territory with young women.

After breakfast, registration and equipment check, each player had been assigned a coach and field times, both morning and afternoon. Geoff—being the newbie, he suspected—had the earliest morning time but his afternoon field slot was a full two hours after lunch, leaving plenty of time for drills between field play on the beautifully tended pitch of soft green turf. He decided to begin the daily warm-up with an easy jog through the surrounding forest before hitting the field, something he did frequently when he played professionally to get himself centered and to clear his mind before stepping onto the pitch.

He was glad to find that the towering redwoods shaded the practice area in the afternoon, minimizing the risk of heatstroke, but even so, the days were warm and the nights chilly. The food was good and plentiful, the showers warmest if you got there first, and the training exhausting. His girls strove to achieve excellence to ensure themselves successful trials for their varsity teams in middle or high school the coming fall. This relatively new American sport was gaining recognition as the U.S. Women's Soccer Team became unbeatable, gathering a loyal impassioned following, unlike the men's team.

He found coaching girls a challenge. They seemed to have more compassion for their fellow players and less killer instinct than their male counterparts. They might cry more easily when injured or discouraged, but they came together and supported each other quickly, rarely showing any personal rivalry. After all, the team they emulated had many of the same qualities. He'd adjusted his vociferous, threatening coaching style to something less critical and more encouraging, and the adjustment was clearly paying off. The drills he'd designed fit their strengths and skills, building on their team spirit and camaraderie while not holding back those who showed real promise. His focus initially was on "shadow play"—playing without opponents and an emphasis on controlling the ball as it was received—while staying "tuned in" to the pacing of the game itself. It took the girls some time to understand and accomplish these skills. Once these were introduced, practiced and understood, he moved on to dribbling, using various passing skills. Many of the assistant coaches were amateur players and impressed by his complex repetitive drilling and innovative style. He encouraged the girls rather than critiquing them negatively.

One very pretty blonde coach immediately caught Geoff's eye. She was tall, tanned and a talented ball handler. He made a mental note to find out more about her. Sitting next to Case over cold pasta and veggies he was soon aware that Case's eyes were following the lean muscular legs of "his" blonde. They caught each other's gaze and laughed out loud. "Ah, so many out there to tempt us, and we both gravitate towards the same girl. Not much of a surprise though, is it Case?" Geoff was familiar with the tendency of not only his teammates but also his friends to be attracted to the same type of women, but he knew it mattered little, as the women made their own choices. The ball was always in their court, men still outnumbering women in this sport.

Playing professionally in South America, until a knee injury ended his pro days, had afforded Geoff ample opportunity to play, off the field. The liaisons formed on the circuit had been short but intense. The game had always come first for him, and the women knew it. Settling down never crossed his mind until he'd started to coach and realized aligning himself with one school might be an easier task than going from camps to schools to teams on the rise to city-sponsored programs. But no clear path had presented itself, yet.

At a young age he'd had dreams of his success as a player and he'd never doubted it would come to pass. However, the vision had not included the injury he'd suffered in a play-off game two years ago in Italy. Visions, he knew, were often incomplete or difficult to interpret, but almost everyone in his family accepted them as the guiding light in their lives, never ignoring them. No true revelations had ever been left unfulfilled, or so the stories were told. It struck him that none of his dreams had ever included a woman, then or now.

It didn't take long for the lanky blonde, Josie, to approach him. She'd noticed him that first day but knew from experience that players were a risk to get involved with. She hadn't competed professionally, yet, but still aspired to do just that. Given her own drive, she understood her male counterparts' single-mindedness and accepted the risk of being hurt when they inevitably chose soccer over family. She'd already left behind her own family in Oregon, school and a college boyfriend who couldn't accept her passion. Watching Geoff's drills, she'd found herself incorporating those she was drawn to into her own routine, adapted for her younger players.

Geoff wondered at the similarity of their approach until Case said over lunch, "You have an admirer. She's been watching you and obviously likes your style, since she's adopted your drills. Take it as a compliment? Or the chance for an introduction perhaps?"

On the third night at dinner it was Josie who asked if the seat across from Geoff was open. Case, seated next to him smiled, stood, gestured to his seat and said, "All yours. I'm off to the showers before the hot water's gone."

Their conversation was easy. The topic went from pro soccer teams leading the league, segueing into his competitive days, and then to her desire to turn pro. She readily admitted she'd seen and adapted some of his drills to fit her own coaching regime.

Geoff was struck by her openness and confidence. She seemed to possess down-to-earth views on hard work and success. She'd be well suited for the pro circuit, and he knew her chances would improve if she got a little coaching herself. That might come later, if the time was ever right.

For the next several days they found themselves sharing lunch or dinner, side by side on the long wooden benches set up under the open tents of the mess hall. Case and Geoff continued to exchange coaching ideas and frequently kicked the ball around on the pitch between sessions. They realized over a six-pack of cold beer late one night that their paths to a professional team had been quite different.

Case's father had played football in Australia and encouraged his son with private coaches, Ivy League schools, and opportunities to play with minor league teams. Geoff, on the other hand, had a father who wanted his son to be a lawyer or a doctor, had very little schooling himself, and didn't understand his son's passion for football. If Geoff hadn't had his dreams and his grandmother's belief in him, he might never have succeeded. And succeed he had.

Geoff fell asleep pondering his path to fame and found himself back in the world of dreams he'd known since childhood—visions of success, and also the voices telling him he'd been chosen for great things to come. Long days made sleep easy, but as the weeks wore on, he realized that one dream had become a nightly occurrence. Before coming to the States, this vision had been less frequent, less vivid, although he'd been experiencing it most of his life. It seemed as if he was taking trips to worlds underground inhabited by voices without bodies. It neither surprised nor frightened him. It was simply a curiosity that vanished at dawn.

The visions of playing professional football that had motivated him to train tirelessly—always outdistancing his fellow players by risking injury rather than settling for second best—were not at all the same as this one recurring experience. He sensed that something in the character of this particular vision was changing but he wasn't sure what. He did know that what he saw, or remembered seeing, had become more detailed and more easily accessible upon awakening than it had been before.

He thought about telling his grandmother what he was experiencing, these dreams that wouldn't leave him be, but the memory of her dismissing some of his childhood visions as "just the ramblings of a young active imagination," kept him from reaching out to her. She'd pointed out that, "All dreams are not premonitions. Some are just dreams and deciding, for yourself, which are which, may be difficult." However, his grandmother had been the one to assure him that he was right in believing he would become a famous player for the Argentine National Football Team. Perhaps this dream now was just his imagination, not a real vision at all, but he doubted it seriously. He decided to ask Josie if she dreamed of things that came to pass, hoping to get the confirmation he needed that he wasn't alone.

He felt that there was something magical about living in this forest of giants. The ground was spongy with centuries of decaying needles. The sunlight was filtered but intense where it broke through the tall canopy. The redwood bark was a rich red and easily peeled off in soft layers. Busy, bushy-tailed squirrels made nests in hollows where limbs came together. At night, in the stillness, he could hear the streams running through the forest with their deep pools home to small crawfish and huge water skimmers.

He drifted off to the sound of the stream, with the moon slowly rising, and opened his eyes to the sound of something akin to crashing surf and bright light, as if a car passing had its high beams pointed at his open windows. He tried to turn away but couldn't move. The light was moving towards him slowly, getting brighter. It stopped at the foot of his bed, expanded, and revealed a figure, silhouetted. There was something familiar about this figure. It was built like the man called Ichabod Crane in Irving's *The Legend of Sleepy Hollow*, "tall, but exceedingly lank, with narrow shoulders, long arms and legs, hands that dangled a mile…feet that might have served for shovels…the head…small with… large green glassy eyes…" *Yes, that must be it—the childhood tale had come alive.* Then the head craned forward, the whole figure appearing fluid, and the greeting was voiceless:

We've been with you for a very long time. You've been chosen, were chosen, long ago to know our world. The time has come. We will be back for you soon, very soon.

The head moved out of focus as it returned to the dark silhouette. The light faded as the figure disappeared. Geoff lay motionless, wondering if he was awake or asleep, but the cold air, the discomfort of his sweat chilling him, and his heart racing were not part of just a dream. He grabbed at the down comforter, pulling it up around his neck. Then reconsidering, he ducked his head under the covers. He didn't sleep. He tried to remember everything he could about what he'd been experiencing since childhood. *This world the figure spoke of; had he been there? Did he already know that there was another world? Why was this happening?*

When Geoff woke, Case was already up, sitting across from him on the end of the bed. Looking up he asked, "Geoff, are you alright?"

He didn't really consider the question as he rose up onto both elbows, wrapped snuggly in the comforter, "Why?"

"Well, I'm not sure. It's just that I felt as if someone was in the room with you, with us, last night. It felt…forget it. It's probably just my imagination." Geoff knew Case was right but he wasn't sure how to respond, so he didn't.

Coaching was a welcome distraction. The evening review of practice film footage allowed him to use his expertise to guide and teach, taking his mind off speculation. When lights out sounded across the campus, he was less than enthusiastic about turning in, but he drifted off and slept peacefully—no visions.

The sense that something momentous was happening reinforced his decision to approach Josie. She sat patiently on the grass as he described his childhood dream, the one that had come back again so vividly. When he finished, she remained quiet.

After a bit, she began, "I've never had a dream that recurred, always the same, I mean. I believe you when you say that you do, but I'm not sure if it really means anything. Maybe you want it to be real, but it's something born of your own imagination, something that makes you feel that you're more than a football player. Is there something else you want?"

Geoff was the one who was quiet now. He wasn't sure what he wanted. He'd wanted to be a football player, so that particular dream had been easy to accept and to live with until it came true. But this? Did he want to see more, be more? Did he want to be chosen to know "their world"?

He lay back next to Josie under the stars and all he could say to her was, "All I want right now is you in my arms. I want you close. I want to know that you don't think I'm crazy."

She kissed him gently on the cheek. "Even if you are crazy, and a lot of you players are, I'm okay with that."

He rolled towards her taking her in his arms and laughed. "I can live with that."

For the next few nights Geoff slept uninterrupted—no dreams—and the clarity of what exactly he'd experienced began to fade. Case didn't mention that night again, and Geoff didn't bring it up. Talking to Josie had been enough to help him clear his head, assuring him he most likely was not crazy. The need to explain to anyone else seemed unnecessary and inadvisable, doubting that others would be as unconcerned as Josie was.

The weather was changing, with colder temperatures at night and the scrub oak turning from green to yellow and orange. It was a blustery evening of branches rubbing against the canvas tent, trees swaying in utter darkness and no moon.

Geoff sensed their presence before he saw, this time, two figures silhouetted, standing motionless at the foot of the bed. He felt them in unison.

Now, it's time. Come with us.

His heartbeat was steady this time, his mind unfettered—fearless. He let go of thought completely. The three minds became one. He felt a sense of peace surrounding them as they drifted in the dark. He sensed the feeling of motion without any assurance they were actually moving. The darkness faded to a dim light emanating from the walls of what he thought was a tunnel of rock and dirt disappearing in both directions. They drifted down the tunnel, the wall opening onto smaller rooms off to either side. There were no figures in the dim light, but he sensed the presence of others. Voices without forms came and went. A large cavern opened up around him, and he knew he was in the presence of many. The walls began to glow, and he was surrounded by the same lanky forms he'd seen at the foot of his bed, silhouetted, only this time there were hundreds of them.

Case sat up suddenly, his eyes wide open. The room was awash with light and he could barely make out two figures at the foot of Geoff's bed. He wanted to shout out a warning but wasn't able to find his voice. Then the figures were gone. As the light faded he could see Geoff peacefully breathing, the quilt rising and falling rhythmically. He heard his own voice calling Geoff's name, hoping for…for what?

Geoff bolted upright looking across at Case. He saw the frightened expression, the confusion and disbelief, "I'm okay, really. It's okay." But Case was the one who was not okay. Geoff stood slowly, crossing to his friend's bunk and sat. Case was unsure what he'd actually seen, hoping somehow none of it was real. But Case didn't have many dreams and this wasn't like any he'd ever experienced. He struggled to understand why Geoff was so calm as he was explaining that it wasn't a dream, not really.

"I've been seeing the light and hearing voices most of my life. The figures, the ones you saw, are new. I didn't know anyone else could see them. If I'd known…I don't know, maybe I would have told you about them." Case closed his eyes. He was visibly still shaken and no amount of explanation, right now anyway, would change that. Unlike Geoff, he hadn't experienced any of this before. He hadn't developed the acceptance of events or feelings over time.

At breakfast Case took Geoff aside and told him he wasn't ready to see any more, or hear any more. He wanted to move to another cabin. He made it clear he wasn't afraid of Geoff, but couldn't experience another night like the last one again, ever. He was Catholic. They did believe in miracles and revelations and visions, but he wasn't ready, not yet, and he couldn't recall the Bible describing anything like these creatures. Geoff understood as he watched Case walk away. When he'd "heard" Case call his name the night before, he'd found himself back in the cabin; the light, the cave, the figures— all of it had disappeared. He'd opened his eyes to see his friend's terrified face. There was no changing what had happened, but the fact that Case could see "them" was bewildering.

Josie came up behind Geoff. "Are you two okay? Case didn't look too good." Geoff took her arm and walked her towards the trees.

"He saw some of what I told you about—the light, the figure. He didn't have the dream, the vision that I have. He only saw part of mine. I'm sorry, I don't want to frighten you, and it did frighten Case."

Josie had never considered that the vision could be anything but that—a vision. She wasn't frightened, but then again she hadn't experienced what Case had. She wasn't particularly religious but did consider herself spiritual and open to new ideas or possibilities. Unsure how she could be of any help she said lightheartedly, "Well, at least you know you're not crazy—at least not in the certifiable sense—seeing that someone else can see what you can."

He smiled only slightly, not really able to muster much more than that. They walked in silence. When they started back to the campus, she asked what she'd been wondering, "Are you ready to go with them, if they come again?"

Geoff turned and answered, "Yes. I was last night. I still am. I'm meant to see more."

Case found other lodging easily, and although they still saw each other on the pitch trying out new drills, passing the ball, occasionally sharing their thoughts regarding the end of camp and how best to pursue their passion for the sport, the two never mentioned that night again.

Geoff knew he was ready to see what he'd glimpsed, so this time when he sensed them near, he consciously let his mind drift to the cave and the Others.

He heard them in unison.

We welcome you back among us. Heads bowed slightly and then lifted, the green eyes all focused on Geoff. *We do not exist as actual beings, but once, long ago, we did. Now we can become visible when we choose, in any form we choose. What you see is the physical form we have adopted most often, over many centuries, if we've needed one or wanted one. You've seen us or sensed us for many years now.*

Geoff wasn't hearing a voice or voices but a singular awareness communicating with him.

We've been watching from afar for all time, from a universe beyond your reach. We've walked among you in bodies no different than your own when we've chosen to know you better or to guide you. We are among you even now and mean you no harm. Remember us, and we will be with you if you choose to be with us.

Geoff woke the next morning with a sense of well-being, surrounded by an uplifting presence. His senses were heightened, his vision crystal clear.

He went through the day with inspired insight into each girl's skills, needs and emotions. His own sense of well-being seemed to radiate from those around him; each seemed able to access their own best self effortlessly. The girls shifted from just watching the ball to intuitively being aware of the position of their teammates and passing with rare accuracy.

Josie was able to sense the change in Geoff as well and she let it flow through her and on to others around her. He continued, until camp ended in August, to unconsciously guide those around him to offer up their best.

There were no more dreams until the last night, but he felt their presence with him always, in some way a part of his being. Case had plans to return to Australia, working with the Aussie Football League, and Josie had taken up Geoff's offer to go with him to Brazil where he'd lined up his next job. The girls' football team there would be holding trials soon, and Geoff knew that Josie, with his help, would have no trouble getting an offer to join the League.

The last night in the redwoods was filled with fond farewells and speculation as to what the future might bring, leaving everyone with a sense of promise. As he lay alone in the cabin watching the moon rise, light peaking through the redwoods, the forms appeared, silhouetted, and he found himself once again in the large cavern.

You now know the power you share with us. You have embraced the Way of One, bonding us in harmony and peace, capable of what we can conceive. Those around you who choose, will become what they can dream. You only need think about our presence in your life, and we will appear to you.

Geoff did think of their presence. He asked questions and found that the tunnels and caves physically existed, well below the city and bay of San Francisco. There were other places the Spirits, or Others, as some have called them, choose now or have chosen in the past to appear—in the Himalayas, in Egypt, in the mountains of Peru and in the deserts and oceans of many countries around the globe.

Returning to South America he told his grandmother about his visions—about the Others. She got up from her rocking chair smiling, took his head in her hands and kissed him on each cheek. He knew now that she too had always been one of the chosen.

She ventured, "Many of the greatest spiritual leaders throughout time may have known and embraced the Way of One. She looked up into his eyes, "Each appearance of the Others, both now

and throughout history, has offered—does offer—
an opportunity to be a part of the Way of One.
Giving the gift of realizing your full potential as an
individual, choosing everlasting peace and harmony,
and embracing the thought that all that surrounds us
is part of us, is living the Way of One."

The Magic of Maui

2nd place, 2015 Lahainatown Action Committee Short Story Competition

Nansy Phleger

"Please return to your seats and place your dinner trays in an upright position, as we will be landing shortly. Thank you for flying with Hawaiian Airlines, and we hope you enjoy your stay on Maui."

Fat chance, thought Sarah. *No job due to the company's sale, no boyfriend due to a redhead, now I've gotta spend my holiday doing an online job-search...boy, I sure hope Maui lives up to its reputation as being a magical place, 'cause I could sure use some magic now.*

What a beautiful hotel... she thought as the taxi pulled into the Historic area of Lahaina, *...so close*

to the water and central to all the activities I'd like to do means I won't need a car. Oh, what a lovely room! And a view of the ocean! This is gorgeous. Forget the job search, I'm going downstairs to eat and then spend my day seeing the sights!

Lahaina's busy harbor was filled with people, some arriving from the massive cruise ship lying at anchor just to the south, others waiting for the ferry to take them across the channel to the island of Lanai, most lining up to join various tours offering everything from snorkeling to whale watching to fishing for elusive game fish. Off to one side beneath the shade of an almond tree was a fellow playing an *'ukelele,* while lovely ladies in *mu'umu'us* and *leis* danced and swayed to his sweet melodies.

What a treat this is—everything so colorful and interesting. Sarah followed some folks down the walkway to explore all the possibilities offered, then crossed the little road to discover the Old Courthouse, which held a museum, a wonderful gift shop, and the Lahaina Arts Society, all situated next to the largest old banyan tree she had ever seen. *Well, it all feels special, but I'm not sure if it's really magical.*

Sarah stepped up to the rocky breakwater to watch locals teaching tourists how to surf. Some were doing really well, while others repeatedly toppled into the shallow water, popping up through the foam laughing, enjoying themselves regardless.

Something caught Sarah's eye farther down the beach, so she climbed over the rocks, removed her sandals and walked in the shallow water, then up the sandy slope to reach an older woman wearing a colorful *mu'umu'u,* sitting on the short wall under a large tree, busily pulling, folding, and tucking blades of greenery into a sort of circular braid.

"Aloha," the woman said, smiling. "How are you enjoying our lovely island of Maui?"

"So far, it's really nice, though I've only just arrived this morning."

"What made you choose to come here?"

"Well, originally, this was to be my annual job holiday, but the company got bought, so now it's part of my severance package, and my boyfriend was going to come with me, but he took off with his coworker, so I came anyway."

"Oh, all good news, yeah? Best way to start your life on the island," she smiled.

"How's all this good news?"

"Because now the old stuff gone, you have plenty space for good stuff, like better job, better boyfriend, someone without wandering eye, yeah?"

"Well, I did hope to get some of that magic Maui

is famous for, but I'm not sure where to look for it."

"The magic of Maui is all around—above, below, but mostly in—everything. You'll see. Here," she said, handing the braided greenery to Sarah.

"Wow, it's a hat! That is so cool! Can you teach me how to make one?"

"Sure, come tomorrow, same time, I teach you then. Aloha, *a hui hou.*"

Sarah walked down the beach, happy with her new hat. She turned to wave a thank you, but the old woman had left the beach. Sarah waded in the shallows again, enjoying the cool water, noticing the little fishes darting from sun to shadow in little schools. Ahead of her was a fisherman, casting his lure into a deep blue area, then waiting patiently for the pole to tip.

"Any luck?" she asked.

"Yeah, but the wind took my hat, so I'm 50-50 now," he smiled.

"Here, now you're 100 percent again," Sarah smiled and handed him her hat.

"*Mahalo nui loa.* Thank you very much, now here's your dinner," he said, reaching into his ice chest pulling out a large shiny fish and handing it to her. "My uncle came by earlier, and gave this to me."

"What is it?"

"*Ono.* That means it's delicious, but it's also its name. Enjoy!"

"Thank you, and good luck," said Sarah, heading off down the beach dangling her large shiny fish.

"What you got there, girl? A little something-something for the grill?" A tall Hawaiian man stood next to a barbecue grill at the top of the grassy bluff, a long spatula in his hand. Next to him people were setting up chairs and filling long tables with bowls and platters of food. "You are just in time. Come along, fill your plate, but first we join hands, say prayer to bless the meal."

Sarah did as she was told, enjoying the food and friendliness of this lovely group of locals who made her feel so welcome. Then a shout, chairs tipped, a rush to one end of the long table.

"He can't breathe!"

"Someone help him!"

Sarah jumped into the cluster of heads and flailing arms, yelling, "Stand back, give me room," grabbed the teenager from behind, clenched her hands into a fist, then jerked her fists into him, then again. Then the third time, out shot a chunk of meat.

"He's breathing!"

"Color coming back!"

"Sit down, boy!"

"Next time no talk till mouth empty, hear?" Everyone was talking at once, some still fussing over the embarrassed kid, but most now meeting Sarah, thanking her for her help, asking where she was from, and how she had learned the Heimlich maneuver that had saved the boy's life.

"I was the marketing manager for a company that just got sold, so I'm jobless now, but I'm also a trained paramedic. I usually volunteer during emergencies."

"Could I speak with you for a moment?" A tall, good-looking fellow took her arm, gesturing to some chairs off to the side. "I've inherited a little hotel here, and need to do a lot of work to make it a viable business, you know, restoration, decorating, gardens, and once that's done, I'll need to get a marketing plan set up. Do you do that sort of thing? Could I offer you a job? I mean, a paramedic would be a real asset to my little hotel, too."

"Yes, I'm very interested, but first I'd like to see your hotel. Tomorrow morning, 11 a.m.?" Sarah took his card and shook hands, then went to say good-bye to everyone at the luau, checking one more time on the teenager.

"I'm fine now, thank you very much. My mom

wants to know if you'd like to go whale watching with us, maybe tomorrow, about 3 p.m.? She'll bring food so we can stay out till sunset, and I promise to have better manners!"

"How wonderful, that is so kind of you. I'll be here at 3:00."

The next morning Sarah walked quickly down the beach, past all the surfers and tourists enjoying the sun and sand until she once again reached the old woman beneath the shady tree, weaving hats from palm fronds.

The old woman greeted her warmly. "Aloha. You are happier today than yesterday. Ready to learn how to make a hat?"

"Yes," Sarah replied. "Weave a hat, catch a fish, maybe even how to hula, sing, and surf, because everyone and everything—all of it—is a part of the Magic of Maui."

Most Embarrassing, Long Remembered

Nansy Phleger

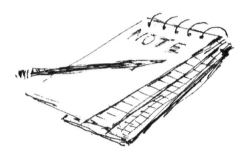

I was seventeen, had recently earned my driver's license, and was always eager to run errands for anyone who needed milk, or eggs, or whatever just so I could get behind the wheel of our family's 1958 two-tone Chevy, turn the radio dial to *the* rock and roll station, up the volume to the appropriate "cool" level, roll my window down to nonchalantly rest my left arm, and cruise Tustin, California, covering about two miles from our house to the new shopping center where the supermarket optimistically sat at the far end of a massive stretch of striped asphalt.

I aimed for the farthest reaches, zipping along over the zebra patterns, oblivious to the sparse cars dutifully parked within the stripes, selected a spot on the far side, and properly parked.

Then I was approached by two middle-aged men (they could have been in their thirties, but looked old to me), one holding up his hand, both looking at me with serious intent, so I stayed put until they stood before me. Neither of them said a word.

I watched while the fellow who had raised his hand withdrew a small notebook and a pencil from his pocket, and began writing something, no one saying anything, me just watching the man write, the other man watching me watching the man write.

Then he ripped off the paper and handed it to me, both watching as I read, "We are deaf mutes who are horrified at how fast you drove through this parking lot with total disregard for the possibility of other drivers backing out or pedestrians suddenly emerging from their cars. You must learn to drive more slowly and safely. Do you understand?" Then with wagging heads and waving a finger of admonishment, they turned and left.

I was hot with embarrassment, humiliated at having to stand still while he wrote, and mortified at being scolded without a sound being made.

I've never forgotten his silent message, though it has been almost sixty years since he kindly took the time to teach a teen.

Mobile Phone

Nansy Phleger

Hi, Sylvia, it's me, Laura. I'm running a bit late, sorry...

Last client wanted to talk, you know how it goes. Once the Living Trust is sorted, they want to explain their decisions. Mr. Samuels is very wealthy, but also very lonely...

No...I couldn't rush him...he's a sweetie.

(Laughing) Don't be silly. I'm younger than his daughters...more like his granddaughters...two... never sees them though...yep, very sad.

We chatted over tea and cake, then I sent him home with cookies I'd made. Yep. Next week, after

I get the papers typed up...says he wants to fix me up with his nephew...hey, could be good...only if he's as nice as Mr. Samuels.

OK, I'm out the door, heading down the hall.

So the new pub is really fun, huh? If you say so! I could use some flirty fun on a Friday night, that's for sure. Elevator's here, see ya in 15...

Ciao!

●　●　●

Sylvia! Oh, my God, you won't believe...

(Mumbling, breathing hard, phone hits a hard surface)...I'm trying...

(Now shouting...) are you SURE they're coming?

(Breathless) Sylvia, I got attacked! Yes! In the elevator. This guy just lunged at me...from behind!

Oh, my God, my worst nightmare!

Yes...I remembered...inhale, crouch, smashed my elbow right into his...oh, gotta go, the ambulance is here.

Because he's out cold on the floor, that's why!

(Shouting) Over here...YOO-HOO! Yes, this man!

(Whispering) Good Lord, how many men do they see on the lobby floor!

Later, Syl!

. . .

Hi Syl, me again...uh-huh...to Admitting...the hospital! Because they made me climb into...ye-ah! Major scene...sirens, speeding, swerving, chest thumping with those huge paddles...terrifying!

Because they gave me his personal effects... wallet, keys...probably thought I was his wife...uh-huh...I have to...yep, weird, but if I don't, who will?

(Puffing a bit) I'm running down the stairs. No, no more elevators today, thank you! Almost there...

Well, paramedics said heart attack...I said nothing...except at first, when I'd told them he'd jumped me.

No, he's not old...uh-huh...ummm, dark...dark hair...looked sorta long...

GROSS! I did NOT do mouth-to-mouth...are you crazy, Sylvia?

OK, now I'm in line...hold on...here's his license...name's...FERGUS! My God, who'd name their defenseless baby *Fergus? Fergus James Mitchell*...hmm...born two years before me...quite young!

Uh-oh!

Sylvia, he lives in my building...uh-huh...the

perv's a neighbor!

What do you mean, "maybe he's not a thug?"

Oh, here's his health insurance card...oops, I'm next, gotta go.

• • •

Me again, Sylvia. Looks like I won't be joining you at the pub...oh, is it fun? Sounds as though it's getting a bit raucous...

Who's that singing? Is it always that...it is? Gosh. Well, have a beer for me. I could use a shot of Scotch, but reckon the vending machines don't stock that.

Yep, a private room...called his mum...next of kin...sure...very upset. Hobart...gets in tomorrow... noon...a widow.

Nope, not this time...such a bummer. Let's plan on next week, OK?

Me? I'm heading to the hospital's cafe...

Why? I'm starving, it's almost ten, and I've been a little too busy to...

Oh...because the doctor wants to see me. Not sure, pretty busy here...yep...probably understaffed, too.

(Whispering) I really need to see the doctor, Sylvia! Because I'm worried I nearly killed him!

Yes!

Think about it. What if he were really having an heart attack, and then...uh-huh! I just went all *Kung Fu Katie* and whomped him in the gut...If I burst something, some vessels, I'd be...right, responsible!

(Normal voice) Syl, I was thinking more about... karma?

(Now hissing) Because beating up a sick man is not good, is it?

(Thinking) No, I don't think he'd sue...wait, do you think he'd sue me?"

(Shrieking whisper) Oh, my God! He could! My life would be shot to…

(Suddenly normal voice) Cafe's busy...Hey, hot food! I'm in heaven! I'll call later, Sylvia...have another umbrella drink for me, OK?

Ciao!

• • •

Sylvia? That you? I didn't know you could sing! No, you sound good...a little slurry...not bad...really!

No...nope...no way! No karaoke for me. Uh-uh.

Because I don't enjoy public humiliation! A shower singer, that's me.

In his room...still waiting on the doctor. It's alright, it's not like I have anything exciting going on in my life...

Of course, except the pub, but now it's nearly midnight so I've missed that.

Yep...it's nice, for a hospital. Has a big window...city looks really beautiful from up here...fifteenth...

You're waving? All of you? How many are...? That's so funny!...Sure, I can see you...can even hear you all, too! Hah, you wish!

Uh-huh...has its own bathroom, too, which is a godsend, I'm telling you!

A big, comfy chair, and an extra pillow and blanket, so I'm OK.

Next to him...he's sleeping...he's actually cute...uh-huh...

Looks peaceful, but that could be due to the drugs...

Of course...machines, tubes, monitors, nurses...everything here but the doctor...sheesh!

Oh...the pub's closing? What? Who's going? God, I love that deli! I could kill for their hot pastrami on rye with those massive garlic dills... oops, shouldn't say 'kill'...sounds bad, you know... with the guy lying here, still out cold...

What do you mean, how big are his hands and feet?

(Gasping) OH!...Good heavens!

Syl-vi-ah! How rude! I can't believe you're saying that!

(Giggling) No, I will NOT peek!

(Giggling and snorting) Stop it!

(Wheezing) You're making me laugh so hard I can't breathe!

(Whispering) Oh no, a nurse heard me and peeked in and scowled, can you believe that? Like, I'm in summer camp or something!

(Composed) Ahem...he has lovely hands, actually...um-hmm.

Because I'm holding one of them, that's how... No, I haven't searched for his feet...

(Sternly) and I'm not going to, so just behave yourself, girlfriend!

Jeez, who's yelling for you? Oh, I know him... uh-huh...no, he's nice...it's just...he's usually so quiet...

Guess you just bring out the beast in him...uh-huh...you and José Cuervo!

You're having so much fun...no...you deserve it, especially after that creep Jeffrey...the bum...

He's whistling! A passionate guy...who knew?

OK, enjoy the deli...I've gotta get some sleep anyway.

G'nite, Syl.

. . .

Good morning, Sylvia, it's Laura, and I...oh... well...call me back, OK?

. . .

Hi Syl, it's Laura and...oh...call me soon, OK?

. . .

Sylvia? It's 11 am, for Pete's sake! I need to talk with you! Wake up!

. . .

Hello! Are you ever going to get up? It's almost noon and I have...well, it's about time!

What?...oh...really?...he did?...my goodness... oh, isn't that nice...no, Sylvia, I mean it...he's a very nice fellow, very sincere...handsome, too...uh-huh...

Yes, well, Jeffrey will be stunned...the loser... serves him right! I'll think of you having a picnic while I sit here, facing the Inquisition...

Yes and no.

Yes, the doctor came to see Fergus, and no, I didn't speak with him.

Because it was the crack of dawn and I was

sound asleep...uh-huh...snoring loudly…so I've been told...

Nurse didn't want to wake me, thought I needed my rest...yep...probably drooling all over the pillow, too...so embarrassing.

Can't go home...huh-uh…nurse said the doc wants to meet with me when Fergus' mother arrives... yep, between the rock and the hard place, that's me.

I'm too nervous...I got to the cafe about eight, when I tried calling you the FIRST time...the phone is loud?

Sorry...I know, you poor thing...everything's great till the hangover hits....uh-huh...you'll be fine, aspirin works fast...uh-huh...blue...wear your light blue dress...because then your face won't look so red...or green...or whatever!

What were you drinking? Ooh, those are tasty killers!

Well, nurses must be finished poking and probing and bathing by now. May as well return to Fergus' room to await my fate.

OK...I promise. I'll call after it's over, Syl...

Thanks. Bye.

• • •

Sylvia! You are NOT going to believe...are you

sitting down?

Yes, his mother's nice. Lovely…Lenore.

Well, I'm trying, aren't I?

She introduced herself…yes, Fergus was awake, very happy to see her...

No, wait…Sylvia, this is the important part… it's why I called you, for Pete's sake!

So there we are, waiting quietly, all on edge… well, I was, I can tell you that…uh-huh. Then WHOOSH! In walks the doctor, who's about my dad's age...

(Impatiently) It's important because age can mean experience, right? Right, so listen to me...

Lenore and I sit down to watch the doctor slap these X-rays on the light-screen and begin explaining what we are supposed to be seeing...yeah, organs, bones...I'm getting to that!

I tell you, Sylvia, by that time, I was a nervous wreck. I thought at any moment he was going to turn to me and say...

(Lowered voice) "He would have been just fine if you hadn't whomped him in the gut, but you did, and now he needs surgery..."

No!...Wait!...Listen!...

The Doc turns to Lenore and me and says

(Lowered voice) "Fergus seems to have had a

heart attack..."

(Normal voice) I know...myocardi—something, something...don't interrupt, please, Syl...

(Lowered voice) "...in the elevator, and it appears that at the moment his heart stopped beating, he fell forward on to the young lady, who swiftly struck him in the chest, restarting his heart, then she called for the ambulance. Due to her fast action, there is almost no permanent damage that we can see."

Can you believe that, Sylvia? I didn't...yes! I actually saved him!

His mom hugged me...Fergus, too...we all cried...I'm still very emotional...yes...it's been a long, what, not even 24 hours? I'm gobsmacked!

A few more days, just to make sure...a big relief, I'm telling you! We were all scared...for different reasons, of course...but still...

Lenore and I are going to dinner, her treat, she says, isn't she a sweetie?

OK, have a wonderful picnic...I'll call you tomorrow.

Bye-bye, Sylvia!

· · ·

Hi, Sylvia, it's me, Laura...

Oh, you're there! How was your picnic...a

carriage ride? That is so romantic! Today? No, haven't seen that movie, supposed to be good, though...uh-huh...ooh, that's a lovely restaurant, yes...been once.

This has been some weekend, hasn't it, Syl? I mean, for both of us...definitely life changing.

We had a lovely dinner...uh-huh…Italian...nice not to have to eat alone, you know? Lenore is really gracious...funny, too!

Today we're going shopping...says he needs sheets and towels...yep, she likes my place, says it's charming...we had drinks here before…

Likes my home office, too. Says that's smart, saves money...Scotswoman.

Today? I meet with Mr. Samuels, review his Living Trust with him and have him sign it...I've asked Lenore to be the witness.

Oops, there's the buzzer.

Later, Syl.

• • •

Sylvia? Is that you? Why are you giggling? Oh, well, say "hi" to him for me.

I won't be a second...remember yesterday Mr. Samuels had to sign his Living Trust and Lenore was to be the witness? You'll never guess! They dated in high school!

Truth!

Lost touch during Gap Year, but always wondered...

No mobile phones in those days!

Today? They're making up for lost time...

Oh, me? Visiting Fergus again...diet and exercise...I'll make sure he keeps...

Oh, it will be my pleasure, girlfriend!

Enjoy your movie and dinner date!

Bye, Sylvia.

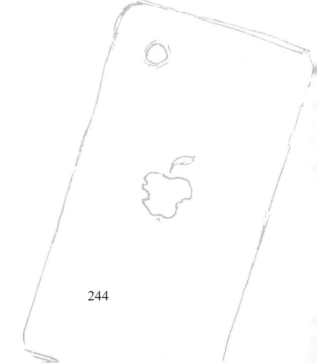

Ain't It Ironic

Nansy Phleger

OK, here's the deal, I'm into funny business. Seriously—I get paid to write jokes for other guys to tell, you know: radio, TV, whatever—so I'm always trying to come up with an idea that can make me some dough, right? It's not that I need much, being young and single, but it's New York, what can I tell you, it costs to do business here.

So last Thursday I get home late and realize I forgot to take out the trash in time to get collected. It's not such a big deal as I don't generate much, except for the dog shit.

See, I have a dog. Actually, it's my Grannie's

dog, but she had to move into Assisted Care, so I took in "Bitsy" and as you can tell by her name, she's not big. She's got some years, same as Grannie, and really is no trouble, really. Bitsy and I visit Grannie every Sunday, and I tell you that dog knows we're going before I even reach for the leash, she's that smart. So I've gotten used to having her, and she's real good about using the minuscule backyard to relieve herself.

So Bitsy and I zip down the stairs for her to do her thing while searching for vermin among the shards of snow beneath the bushes, and after ten minutes or so, she's ready to dash upstairs to warmth. Me too, but I still gotta dump the trash, so once she's settled, I grab the bag, wrap my muffler over my hoodie, and trot down the stairs again and out into a very cold night. Eleven o'clock and there are still people walking home from theaters and cafes, so I decide to trot farther afield with my bag. Oh, I gotta explain about my bag.

See, I got some great mates from high school days, and they're all funny, too. Really funny, I mean it. Anyway, they threw me a twenty-first birthday bash that broke the records, know what I mean? Well, one of their gag gifts was a whole stack of brown paper bags imprinted with a massive dollar sign. They said since I was goin' to take my humor to the Big Smoke, there'd be no wallet big enough to carry my cash, so they gave me bags to carry it all. See? I told you they're funny. I'm not tellin' them that I often use the bags to store Bitsy's poopie sacks before tossing them into the trash can downstairs, which I forgot to do earlier today, which is why I'm hunting down an unlocked dumpster on a side street with no observers. You can get a $500 fine for unauthorized use of someone's dumpster. Seriously, happened to Larry, but that's another story.

So I'm moving pretty quick searching for the perfect place and opportunity when I notice the side street with the street lamp busted right over a dumpster, and figure I am in luck! I check both directions, see a motor scooter coming my way on that dark side street, but figure he'll be past me by the time I toss my sack of crap into the bin, so I start across at a fast clip.

Then I notice he's slowing down a bit, but no problem, I just stay steady—then I notice he's coming toward me and now we're on a collision course. I start windmilling, you know, flailing arms and legs, swinging my sack of shit—with the dollar sign— just trying to dodge this guy and not get smashed in the alley. I mean, what a way to go, right? Well, the scooter dude grabs the sack and speeds away. I am stunned. Stopped short. Then it hits me that guy's gonna look in that sack and when he realizes what he stole, he's gonna be mad, and come looking for me to get whatever he can as retribution.

So I start running, pull off the muffler, toss it in a bush, unzip the hoodie, tie the arms around my waist, gotta look different while sprinting to the safety of home. I'm up the stairs, into the apartment, locking the door, and have turned off all the lights before peeking out the drapes to see Scooter-Dude come around the corner, all slow and easy, swinging his helmeted head from side to side, obviously looking for the guy who made a fool of him.

Yeah, it's a funny story. I can say that now my heart has resumed its normal beat. But you know what's ironic? It's a funny story I cannot sell. Can't make a dime off my near-death experience, or that guy will hunt me down for sure.

A Knock at the Door

Nansy Phleger

"Crikey! Why can't these people keep to the right?" grumped Emma as she dodged and wove her way through the crowds so typical of New York's Fridays. "They have no sidewalk manners!" Two more blocks of delis, sidewalk cafes, and art galleries till she could turn the corner to head down her block, at last sighting the big tree that lent some grace to the old converted warehouse she called home. Stepping into the sudden peace of polished floors and waxed mahogany, Emma paused, closed her eyes, and inhaled the sense of order that prevailed.

"Good evening, Miss Emma, rough week?"

"G'day, Gino, the usual, I reckon. Last Friday of the month is 'Deadline Day,' so too many blokes spittin' the dummy for my liking."

"They're spitting?"

"Oh, sorry, Aussie expression—means temper tantrums, like a baby's. I had thought being a commercial artist in New York would be interesting, but it's just a repetitive and boring routine," Emma sighed. She opened her mailbox, saw it empty, and clicked it closed. "Just like my life," she mumbled.

"What is that delicious aroma?" she sniffed. "Is Mrs. Levin baking again?"

"Yes, of course, and today she told me it's a new recipe for bread." Gino opened his door labeled *Supervisor* then paused, "Before I forget, we got a new tenant for the loft across from you, but the key broke in the door, it's so old, y'know, so I'm waiting on the locksmith, but I gotta go get Maria at her mother's, so if he gets here before I get back..."

"No worries, mate," she called over her shoulder as she trudged up the stairs, "just stick a note on your door directing him to mine."

"Thanks. Mrs. Levin said she'd answer the buzzer for the locksmith."

Emma unlocked her bright red door thinking, *I painted this to be cheery and welcoming, but perhaps it just says "Stop."*

She tossed her keys into the bowl by the door and entered the spacious loft that held a different purpose in each of its corners: kitchen, bathroom, bedroom, and lounge room, all surrounded by tall windows overlooking the city, checked her phone for messages—none—and then changed into her favorite jeans and T-shirt before putting the kettle on for tea and opening the refrigerator to search for dinner possibilities. *Hmm, eggplant, mushrooms, parsley, heaps of tomatoes, some onions and garlic. Guess I've got everything I'll need for a vat of pasta sauce, then I can freeze several packs for later use.*

She poured olive oil into a big pot and began slicing the vegetables as her tea brewed when she heard a knock at the door. *Oh, must be the locksmith* she thought as she turned the heat to low and crossed the room to answer the door. She opened it expectantly but, seeing no one, began to close the door when something big and black flashed past her face and someone spoke!

"Good evening, mademoiselle."

"Aiiieee," shrieked Emma, jumping backwards and clutching her chest. She looked down to see a very short well-dressed man balancing his very tall top hat on the end of his walking stick. He bowed before speaking in a strong French accent.

"Bonjour, mademoiselle. My good friend, Jacob Anderson, is a resident of this building, no? Could you assist me in locating my friend, s'il vous plaît?"

"Oh, sorry, mate, you startled me! Come in, I've got to stir the veggies before they burn. I reckon the bloke you're looking for is the new tenant moving in today across the hall, but he's not here yet. Would you like a cuppa?"

"If that is tea, ma chérie, I'd love a cuppa." The small gentleman placed his top hat and walking stick next to the kitchen stool before perching himself upon it. He took his tea, and watched as Emma added more veggies to the pot.

"That's quite a trick you have with your hat," she smiled.

"Oui, it is a most effective method to become visible. It works beautifully in crowds, as people become alarmed by a floating hat, and I may move with ease."

Emma stirred in the chopped tomatoes, then said, "You sound as though you are far from home."

"Oui, my wife and I arrived from Paris just recently for this opportunity to work with Mr. Anderson. He is director and producer of a cabaret featuring the music I compose. We open in six months, maybe nine, like our little baby." He smiled at his little joke. "But you are not American, no?"

"I'm from Australia, Tasmania, actually, and I've been here about a year on a two-year work permit. I'm an artist, mainly a commercial artist for a small advertising agency not far from here."

A knock at the door interrupted their chat.

"Oops, there's the door. Could you just stir the pot for me? That's probably the locksmith. Mr. Anderson's door needs a new lock, seems there's a key stuck in the existing one, so no one can get in."

Emma set off for the door again, this time making a point to look down first, where she spied large brown feet with bright red toenails in strappy silver sandals, and followed the slim legs upwards into a flowing emerald green silk caftan draped off the shoulders of a tall, brown, beautiful woman with the biggest smile defined by bright red lips; the entire vision topped by a hat of arching plumage. She was simply stunning.

"So sorry to bother you, my dear, but I am looking for Mr. Jacob..."

"Anderson?" Emma finished, "he's not here yet, but please come in..."

"Precious!" cried the little Frenchman from across the room. "You are exquisite as always. Come kiss me and make my wife jealous."

"Pierre, how delightful to see you again, it has been too long. I should have known you'd be the first arrival when a beautiful young lady is involved," the tall woman smiled at Emma, then glided across the room to exchange kissy cheeks with Pierre before asking, "What are you making? It smells divine. Why the aroma simply carried me up the stairs!"

"Pasta sauce, and now it's time to add the mushrooms and zucchini."

"Oh, please let me do that. I love to cook, and I've been deprived being on the road." She washed her hands and fetched an apron.

"Precious is our chanteuse. She lives in my mind as I compose the music."

Another knock at the door, so Emma left the two friends chatting, chopping, and stirring to cross the room, muttering, "That must be the locksmith now."

A burly man in uniform stood before her holding a clipboard.

"I got a piano for Jacob Anderson in 2B, but no one's there. Can you take it?"

"A piano?"

"The piano!" cried Precious and Pierre in unison. "It's here, how wonderful!"

"But how do we get it up the stairs?" asked

Emma.

"No problem, lady. We got a crane, can pull it through the old loading dock over there," pointing to the massive doors that served as backdrop for the lounge room. "They open in," he said as he began moving sofas and chairs aside, then sliding bolts and pulling pegs to ease the doors in and back against the walls, fully exposing Emma's loft to the entire city. "OK, Jack, back 'er up, we're set to go," he hollered down to his team waiting below.

The truck bearing the crane and its heavily wrapped cargo shifted into reverse, then slowly lumbered backward into the alley, easing to a halt beneath the gaping space above, where four curious faces peered in anticipation.

"OK, Jack, you got it perfect. Andy, grab a hold of the hook there...that's it...yeah...looks centered... that's it...OK...when you're ready..."

A knock at the door startled Emma. "Aha," she thought, "surely that's the locksmith..."

"Hello, dear, what's going on? I just had to come see what's happening...here's some bread for you... still warm," shoving the loaves into Emma's hands as she rushed past to see the action out the windows.

"Hi, Mrs. Levin. Come in, meet Precious and Pierre. We're getting a piano through the window, and thank you for the bread."

"A piano! How exciting! I love pianos," gushed Mrs. Levin, squeezing herself between Precious and Pierre. "Nice to meet you both. Is it your piano?"

"Ours to enjoy, my dear," smiled Precious. "We're putting together a new cabaret. Pierre writes the songs and I sing them, and Jacob directs and produces, so it's really his piano."

"He's the new tenant who hasn't shown up yet, which is a good thing actually, because the locksmith hasn't arrived to replace the broken lock," explained Emma while she placed the loaves of warm bread on the kitchen table.

"OK, Jack, start 'er up!" hollered the burly guy, and the crane creaked and clanked into action, the hook pulled taut, the engine strained into full throttle, and the piano began its ascent, dangling momentarily outside the loft like a massive bird before being caught and guided through the dock to settle on the floor inside. "We got it, get ready for the cables," he shouted down, as he quickly dismantled the hook and cables, unwrapped the cargo, bundled the quilts into the cables, attached them to the hook, and then set the lot of them out the window to be winched back down to the truck. "Almost done here," he said as he shut the massive doors, slipped bolts and pegs back into place, and replaced the sofas and chairs. "Who's gonna sign for the piano?"

"I shall," Pierre stepped forward and signed with a flourish as Emma showed the delivery man out the door, then turned to see Pierre and Precious removing a large rectangular object wrapped in brown paper off the top of the piano.

"It is the piano bench, but I'm not sure why it is so bulky and heavy," Precious said, as all four people helped to lower the bench to the floor, where they began unwrapping it. Then they all began talking at once.

"Wine!"

"How clever of Jacob to let the crane do all the work!"

"Two cases of red, one of white. Oh, nice choices, too."

"Quick, the corkscrew. We must taste them!"

"Yes, to christen our piano. It will bring us luck!"

They chose the red, sniffed the bouquet, offered toasts to all, and drank.

"Lovely," they all agreed.

Then everyone moved about, Pierre to stir the sauce, Emma to locate the pasta in the pantry, Precious to slice the warm bread, leaving Mrs. Levin to inspect the piano, first sitting upon the bench, then lifting the lid from the keys, she began to play—softly at first, a bit of Brahms, then—with more courage, a little Liszt,—before bashing into full-blown Beethoven! Mouths hung open as everyone turned to see the little grandmother, eyes closed and smiling, swaying slightly above the keyboard, coaxing melodies to flow forth with ease and mastery.

When she finished, no one spoke. No one could. They gave a collective sigh, and then all began to babble at once.

"Oh, so beautiful!"

"Exquisite!"

"How do you know...?"

"Where did you...?"

Mrs. Levin sat smiling, hands folded in her lap. "I was a concert pianist before I was married," was all she said.

A staccato knock at the door was barely audible above their clamor, and Emma thought, *Oh, I forgot about the locksmith.*

A lovely older man stood smiling at her. "I must be at the right place, because the music of an angel floated me upstairs to your door."

"Yes, you're close enough, mate, but it's really the door over there."

"I'm not hearing your piano?" he asked, peeking past Emma to see the chattering trio beyond.

"Well, that is our piano, rather my neighbor's, but that's the door that needs fixing," pointing across the hall.

He turned to look, then shrugged, "You want that I should fix a door?"

"Isn't that what you do?"

"No, no," shaking his head and chuckling, "I'm Sam Goldman, the piano tuner. Mr. Anderson called me last week and made an appointment for today."

"Oh, sorry, please come in."

Mr. Goldman approached the piano, or more specifically Mrs. Levin, with joyful reverence. "My dear, could that have been you I was hearing? Please allow me to tune this instrument, the better to show off your skill and your passion." Then he lifted the polished mahogany to reveal the hammers and strings and set to work while Mrs. Levin kept a smiling watch.

Pierre returned to stirring the pasta sauce, Emma put Precious to making a big green salad while she filled a cauldron with water and set it on the stove for the pasta. Just as she reached for plates, there was a knock at the door.

"OK, that has just got to be the locksmith."

259

"Gino, Maria, how are you?"

"Fine, we're back now, but I'm guessing the locksmith hasn't been here?" Gino and Maria were both peering past Emma to see Pierre, Precious, Mrs. Levin, and Mr. Goldman all happily engaged and gossiping like old friends. "You're having a party? Can we come, too?"

"Sure, we're all keeping occupied until the locksmith shows up and the new tenant isn't here yet either, so we reckon we'll eat the pasta and salad. Mrs. Levin brought bread, and we've got lots of wine," Emma noticed a couple of bottles of red had already found glasses.

"Oh, I can bring the antipasto: olives, salami, some cheese you'll like—I been there today—even the spicy artichokes, so good! I'll be right back."

Maria met everyone and helped set out the plates, silverware, and napkins, and soon Gino returned laden with flowers and platters of antipasto, which he began passing around the room, encouraging everyone to taste all the various spicy items. "By the way," he said, "I gotta message on my machine. The locksmith is stuck in traffic but will get here 'soon come,' he says."

"'Soon come?'" said Precious. "There's an expression I haven't heard in too long! More wine, m'dear, red or white?" she asked as she glided around the room, plumage bobbling upon her head.

Mr. Goldman, finished with the tuning, began playing a series of Broadway show tunes with Mrs. Levin and Precious lustily singing the lyrics.

Emma saw that the water was now boiling, so she began to add the dry pasta, a little at a time, when there was another knock at the door. "Maria, could you please see who that is? I am in the middle here, and that could be the locksmith."

Maria put down the flowers she had been arranging and bustled to the door, opening it wide to a very petite young woman holding a large bakery box and smiling. "Bonsoir, Madame, I am Celeste. Is my Pierre here?"

"Ma chérie," gushed Pierre, as he embraced Celeste, took the box from her hands, and led her into the room to announce, "Ladies and gentlemen, may I introduce you to my bride, Celeste, who has brought us delicious French pastries from her favorite bakery."

Cheers and clapping were quickly followed by more wine being poured, and then Emma tapped her glass, silencing the room once again.

"This evening I am very happy that Mr. Anderson's lock is broken, for it has brought all of you creative and charming people together in my little loft. So your misfortune has become my blessing, and I appreciate that very much. And now, dinner is served."

Emma looked at her usually empty loft to see it filled with happy and diverse people enjoying themselves, and it filled her with joy. "Just like a *ceilidh* back home in Hobart," she thought. "I am so happy, nothing can top this feeling!"

Her reverie was disturbed by a knock at the door, and once again guessing it must be the locksmith at long last, she pulled it open to see a tall, ruggedly handsome man smiling back at her.

"Good evening, I'm Jacob Anderson. I saw the note on the super's door..."

"Jacob, darling!" cried Precious.

"Monsieur, it is about time," added Pierre, pulling the latest arrival into the room and introducing him to each person with dramatic flair, finishing with "...and this is our gracious hostess, Miss Emma..."

"Rae," she said, "Emma Rae," now blushing at having been caught staring with such obvious delight at this gorgeous addition to the gathering. "It's so nice to meet you, and you are just in time for dinner. Let me get you a glass of wine."

Conversation continued as everyone clustered around the table to help themselves to the feast set before them.

Emma stood at the stove to ladle sauce over pasta on the proffered plates, when another knock at the door caught their attention. "That must be the locksmith!" they shouted as one voice, then laughed uproariously at their joke.

"Precious, could you do the honours this time, please? I'm up to my ears in pasta," said Emma smiling sweetly as she served sauce to Jacob Anderson.

"Yes, darlin', I'll see to it," as she floated across to open the door, beholding a very tall, dark, and handsome man, dressed in a colorful Hawaiian shirt. Neither said a word. They just stood smiling at each other.

"Who is it, Precious?"

"I'm not sure, but I am hoping it is my Prince Charming, come to my rescue," drawled Precious.

"I am Clarence Bent, locksmith, at your service, and I would be very honored to be your prince, so that I may make you my princess," he replied, smiling broadly and bowing deeply.

Precious placed her hands on her hips, leaned back and asked, "Where in the Caribbean are you from?"

"Jamaica, m' love, and yourself?"

"I can't believe it. Port Antonio is my home, and yours?"

"St. Thomas Parish, to the south."

"Ahh," she murmured, "where the drums speak."

Emma joined the smiling couple. "I am so glad you finally got through the traffic, but come have dinner first, we're just sitting down."

Precious led her fellow countryman around the room introducing him to everyone before filling their plates and settling on the sofa to learn all they could about each other.

"Thank you so much for your gracious hospitality," Jacob smiled at Emma, seated next to him by the windows. "I was delayed in business meetings with bankers and lawyers...lots of details—they love details!"

"That's where the devil lies, right?" grinned Emma, "Or is that God?"

"It must be God, one of her more clever punishments, perhaps."

The loft hummed with conversations and laughter as dishes were done, coffee and tea prepared, and plump pastries of cream and chocolate were set upon serving trays and passed around the room.

Pierre approached the piano. "Precious, s'il

vous plaît?" he called out as he sat upon the bench, struck three powerful chords to bring all to attention, and then began playing a beautiful, gentle melody. Precious leaned against the piano, smiling, swaying slightly, and waited until Pierre gave a nod, and then she began to sing softly in French, much as a mother would croon to her babe. The song grew in volume and passion, Precious lifting her voice from deep resonance to lyrical soprano, then dropping to an anguished sigh as she finished with a bow of her feathered head.

Silence was followed by raucous applause and shouts of "More!" So Pierre played, Precious sang, and Clarence joined in, thumping and snapping a rhythm from an upended wastebasket. Gino and Maria began dancing and were soon joined by Mrs. Levin and Mr. Goldman. "That leaves just you and me. May I have the pleasure, Miss Emma?"

"I'd be delighted, Mr. Anderson."

"Please, call me Jacob,...and often," he grinned as he swooped Emma onto the dance floor.

The camaraderie continued throughout the evening, with piano players exchanging places with dancers, songs shifting moods from ballads to silly ditties to even a rousing rendition of "Waltzing Matilda" for Emma's benefit before finishing up with everyone singing "I'll Be Seeing You."

Gino and Maria gathered up their antipasto trays, said goodnight to everyone, and went downstairs to their apartment. Clarence attended to the lock, with Precious standing nearby to hand him whatever tool he needed next, and Mrs. Levin invited Mr. Goldman to her apartment to show him the latest photos of her grandchildren. "I was hoping for etchings, but the photos I'll take," he smiled with a shrug as they said their goodnights and headed downstairs

Pierre spoke briefly with Jacob to arrange the week's schedule, kissed Emma's hand as he thanked her for the lovely evening, and then escorted Celeste out the door with a tip of his tall hat and "Au revoir."

Jacob approached Emma, took both her hands in his, saying, "Thank you for hosting us all this evening. Your generosity magnifies your natural beauty. I hope you'll let me return your hospitality."

Emma blushed, protesting. "But you are the ones who've made this evening magical. I'm just happy to welcome you to the neighborhood."

"Yes, and I am very appreciative. But I have a favor to ask. Could my piano stay with you until I can figure out a way to move it into my place?"

"Of course, I'd love to have your piano. No worries, mate!"

Then Jacob was off to pay Clarence, who was going to drive Precious home. As Emma closed her door, she could hear the two Jamaicans giggling and babbling in Patois all the way downstairs and out the main door.

Emma turned to look at her little home, so full of fun just moments ago, now starkly silent. She sighed, then began rearranging chairs and fluffing pillows and sofa cushions as though to restore some sort of order to her life.

She moved about the room, put away the dishes, set the bouquet of flowers on the kitchen table, switched on the bedside lamp, moved back into the lounge area to snap off the table lamps, then stopped short, spun around, and listened.

There it was again, a soft knock at the door.

"Um, is someone there?"

"Yeah, me, Jacob."

Emma opened her door to see Jacob smiling, the door to his loft swung wide, swirling a brandy snifter in each hand. "I was wondering if I could interest you in a christening drink in my too-quiet abode?"

"Yes, I believe you could," smiled Emma, "Give me a moment to get my key," closing her door. Then she whipped around, ran into the bathroom to brush her teeth, swiped some gloss across her lips, fluffed her hair, and shot a spray of perfume to rush through as she dashed back to her door, stopped, took a deep breath, opened, then closed, her bright red door.

"Uh-oh. CRIKEY!"

Ethan's Summer Vacation

2nd place, 2014 Lahainatown Action Committee Short Story Competition

Nansy Phleger

"Want to change your mind and come along?"

"Nah."

"Charles, let him enjoy camp with the other teens."

"Remember to get outdoors occasionally."

"Sunblock! Did you..." Edith lunged for her son's bulging backpack.

"Got it, and a cushy camp! You guys watch out for quicksand!"

Ethan settled by the airplane window, selected music, and watched San Francisco disappear into fog below. *Three months, no chores, just a Maui Computer Camp with geeks like me! Score!*

Sunshine, lilting music, and a soft sea breeze embraced Ethan as he entered Maui's airport, spotting his name on a placard held aloft by a tall Hawaiian man.

"Hi, I'm Ethan. Are you the camp director?"

"Aloha. I'm Kimo Kahana, a high school teacher, or *kumu*," he said, draping an orchid lei and an arm around his shoulders. "*E komo mai*. First time?"

"Yeah."

"Well, that's tough. The others got called, but your phone was cut."

"Why were you calling us?"

"Ah...no camp. Director took the money and run. Child Protective Services asked me to call everyone. Now you're here, we'll have lunch, then get you onto another plane."

"To where?"

"Home, San Francisco, yeah?"

"I can't."

"Why?"

"No one's there."

"Why?"

"My folks are on sabbatical—Papua New Guinea."

"How long?"

"Three months, same as the Computer Camp...I mean, supposed to be."

Kimo stared at the sea, then gave Ethan a broad smile. "Well, my blessing is a *haole!* OK, we gotta hurry, rain on the way."

"Hurry where?"

"My *'ohana,* I'll *hanai* you till your folks return."

"*'Haole, 'ohana, hanai'*...holy cow," muttered Ethan, following the big flower-shirted Hawaiian out of the airport's shade and into the midday heat to where a big pickup truck was parked.

The road to Kimo's was long enough for explanations, and rugged enough for Ethan to realize they weren't headed to any 'cushy computer camp'! The truck bumped around boulders, forded streams, and dodged only the largest potholes before topping a hill overlooking a farm couched in a valley that stretched to the sea. The truck then swung down the hill, rumbled into the rutted driveway, and scattered dust and chickens past barking dogs with wildly wagging tails.

"Is this your 'ohana?"

"This is our farm. 'Ohana, my family," said Kimo, grabbing Ethan's duffel and leading him into a large, sweet-smelling kitchen.

"Luana, meet Ethan, our *hanai* son till his folks

return September 20th."

"Aloha, Ethan," she smiled. "Perfect time to arrive—mango season!"

"Yeah, hope you aren't allergic. I'm Puanani, bring your stuff, you'll share my brother's room. What's that?"

"My laptop," setting the duffel on a twin bed.

"A computer? We have those at school—no hookup out here."

"None?"

"Nah. Dad doesn't want it anyway, 'takes too much time away from life', he says."

"My computer is my life," mumbled Ethan.

The dogs started barking again, this time running for the beach to greet a tall, slim Hawaiian boy carrying a spear and a string of fish.

"Good fishing, Ekolu?"

"Yeah, plenty for dinner, can dry the rest. Aloha!" he smiled at Ethan.

Lunch was carried to a picnic table under a huge mango tree. The family circled the table, joined hands, and bowed heads while Kimo said prayers in Hawaiian, then they all sang in Hawaiian. Ethan had no idea what was said, but took a deep breath and relaxed, filled with a sense of peace.

"I thanked our ancestors for sending you to us,

and asked them to watch over you," explained Kimo. "and to bless our food. Now, some things might be new to you, but we hope you find *ono,* anyway."

"I'll try, but has he been gone long?"

"Who?"

"Ono. What does he look like?"

Everyone burst out laughing.

Luana smiled, "'Ono' means 'delicious,' Ethan."

"Want some POG?" asked Puanani.

"What's POG?"

"Juice—Parrot Or Gecko."

"Puanani, don't tease! It is juice, but it's passion fruit, orange, and guava nectar."

"How about a little *poke?*"

Ethan winced at the thought of getting a poke, but saw Kimo was offering him a bowl of something red. He recognized some onions, but nothing else.

"Poke is raw *ahi* tuna, onions, *limu,* and ground, roasted *kukui* nuts. Ono, try it," urged Kimo. "Try it with some of the roasted breadfruit, and limu, the seaweed Ekolu gathered this morning."

"Thank you for the ono lunch, Luana," Ethan smiled, helping Puanani clear the table, looking ahead to an afternoon in the hammock.

"Get your trunks, Ethan. We've lots to do before evening glass-off," Ekolu called over his shoulder heading towards a shed.

Ethan pulled on his trunks, seeing his reflection in the mirror: tall, skinny, white, topped by a mass of curly red hair. "I look like a match," he groaned, donned a T-shirt, and joined Ekolu at a workbench, where he was separating the fish.

"Grab the knife and the *kala,* bro'."

"This?"

Ekolu looked up. The gangly kid held the unicorn fish by one fin, and the knife like a ping-pong paddle.

"Uh, ever cleaned a fish before?"

"Not really..."

"OK, watch me, yeah?"

Ethan gladly surrendered the fish and knife to Ekolu, who had it scaled, gutted, tailed, and beheaded in a flash. "Slice the belly, save guts and tail for the garden, cut head, save for soup. Man, you're *really* white now!" Ekolu laughed.

Ethan took a deep breath, grabbed the biggest *ulua* and proceeded to gut and fillet it with more gusto than skill, working shoulder to shoulder with his *hanai* brother till all the work was done.

"Now what?" asked Ethan.

"First pick mangoes for Mom and Puanani. Big job ahead, most for Saturday's market, others for drying or jam, but the mushiest we feed the pigs. Then weed the taro patch, clean the barn, milk the cow, and then—surf!" grinned Ekolu.

Ethan followed Ekolu, not knowing whether to be more worried about the pigs, the cow, or the ocean.

"Um, I've never surfed before, Ekolu. I can swim, but…"

"No problem, bro', I'll teach you. You'll love it!"

Ekolu was a very good teacher. He taught Ethan how to wield the twenty-foot-long mango picker, slop the pigs, milk the cow, shovel the barn, wade and weed the taro, and now—the surf lesson.

"The idea is to paddle out to that area where the waves are forming, Ethan. When a big one rises behind you, start paddling like crazy till you feel it lift the board, then jump to your feet and ride it to shore—FUN!"

Fun if you have a death wish, thought Ethan glumly, struggling to paddle the board through the incoming foam.

Ekolu headed out, Ethan following just far enough behind so that every wave that gently lifted Ekolu rolled forward and smashed Ethan, who arrived at the line-up water-logged and wary.

"Turn it! Ready, bro'...good one...AWRIGHT!" hollered Ekolu as he paddled, caught the wave, jumped to his feet, and gracefully danced his board to shore.

Ethan hollered too, but it sounded more like a garbled shriek when he saw the wall of blue, turned, paddled frantically, jumped to a crouch—arms flailing, terrified of being swept to his death—when suddenly the wave turned to foam and he glided to a sandy stop.

"Awesome, dude. Totally AWESOME!"

"I survived, that's what's awesome," gasped Ethan.

Summer slipped past with Ethan an eager student.

Luana taught him to cook *lau lau:* butterfish rolled in pork steak, wrapped in taro leaves, and steamed till tender.

Puanani taught him Hawaiian: "Your butt is *okole,* trash is *opala, pau* means finished, *ono* is delicious, thank you is *mahalo,* and *aloha* is love—for greeting and leaving—always 'love,'" she smiled.

Kimo taught Ethan how to "read" the sea, catch fish by throwing a net, paddle an outrigger canoe, and even how to play the *'ukulele.*

Sundays, neighbors would gather to share food and "talk story," begun with prayer, followed by songs sung to 'ukuleles, always with hula.

September 20th.

Ethan felt torn: excited to see his parents, but sad to leave his hanai 'ohana.

"Come," said Kimo, leading the family to the table beneath the mango tree where they joined hands in a circle, bowing heads. Kimo spoke first in Hawaiian, then English, asking God and the ancestors to bless their hanai son on his journey with hopes he would return soon and often.

"Could you pray that Ekolu attends college with me in San Francisco?" asked Ethan.

"Auwe! Mahalo, bro'!" whispered Ekolu, as Kumu Kimo did just that.

Charles and Edith Anders were stunned to see their tan, muscular, smiling, long-haired son arrive with fragrant leis and bear hugs!

"Mom and Dad, please meet my hanai 'ohana: Kimo, Luana, Ekolu, and Puanani Kahana."

"But your Computer Camp...?"

"Ah, computers take too much time away from life," smiled Ethan.

The Kahanas just smiled, too.

Thoughts Upon Retirement

Nansy Phleger

"Life's a banquet and most poor suckers are starving to death!"
—Rosalind Russell, as Auntie Mame

In early years you wash the dishes,
then on to shopping, chopping,
attending others' wishes
for more sweet, more savoury,
more starch, more flavory
foods.

At first you're hopeful,
moving fast, then slowing,
waiting for the last
to eat
before you, too, begin to choose from
    proffered treats.

But just as you begin to chew,
someone whispers
"Get up, it's Time…
can't you see you're through?"

Artful Living

Nansy Phleger

Life is made of little choices,
remembered shoulds,
and inner voices.

The big decisions draw
most concern,
mistakenly thinking
it's from these we learn
life's lessons.

Instead it's bits and pieces
of daily living,
thoughts of love,
gestures of giving
that flow to form
the who we are.

Though goals give focus,
it's our diurnal routine
that becomes the clay
holding events and scenes
experienced.

When we complete this life's mosaic,
will your choices result in painful rubble?
Or something artful,
glittering,
prosaic?

About the Authors

T. A. Binkley shares her time between Aspen, Colorado, and Lahaina, Maui. She's been a ski pro for 22 years, working with the disabled. Her passions include spending time with her two children, traveling, painting (exhibiting in Lahaina at Kingwell Island Art), cooking and snorkeling. This is her first publishing endeavor.

Jo Ann Carroll immigrated to the Big Island in 1975, from La Cañada, CA, a suburb of Pasadena. She intended to stay a year and luxuriate in the exotic Sandwich Isles, then return to the mainland and get serious about life. It's forty-one years later and she's still here— forget serious.

Lynette Chun navigates her interior landscape with a myopic lens to give voice to her quirky self, discover her culture, examine the meaning of existence, and other sundry matters.

Lisa Downey is co-author and illustrator of the picture book *The Pirates of Plagiarism,* has illustrated several picture books for Arbordale Publishing and is working on a young adult novel. She loves snorkeling and living with the windows open. Find out what she's up to at lisadowney.com or at BanyanTreats Facebook page.

Elaine Gallant lives, loves, and is still surprised that life has landed her in Hawaii. As a freelance writer with a concentration in Creative Writing and a Journalism degree from the University of Central Florida, her work has appeared in *Orlando Magazine, Golf Orlando, Golf for Women, Travelgolf.com,* and other online and print publications. She's now entered the more complicated world of fiction. Catch up with Elaine at info@WestMauiBookClub.com

Oliver Gold is a spirit like you, having a human experience. He is a yogi, a husband, a father, a poet, a writer and a musician. He has published two novels and five music CD's about the romantic, sometimes lonely, crazy adventure of living in a rainbow state of mind. Sample his passion for life at: www.captainbillybones.com

John Noah Hoʻomanawanui Within each of us, is a voice measured through various outlets. As the eleventh child of twelve from my *paniolo*, fisherman, big rig/bus driving father; iWas normally silent. Peacefully silent. To sit and watch was my favorite pastime. My two brothers who were the closest in age to me, on the other hand, were paired with friends who were also brothers the same age. Both could hold a tune and pitch, unlike i. Honestly, iWas relieved because iWas too shy to even speak as a kid. In fact, at 7yrs iCried from nervousness while leading the class in the pledge of allegiance and patriotic song.

Nansy Phleger writes of the adventures of assisting her research scientist husband "Rick," and living in far-flung lands, from Jamaica to Peru to Tasmania, Australia. They became dual citizens of America and Australia in 2009. Nansy has written and illustrated three children's books, a Metaphysical Workbook, and has won awards for both art and writing. www.nansyphleger.com.

Acknowledgements & Mahalos

Lowell Mapes, cover artist

Contributing short story authors

Nansy Phleger, chapter sketch artist

Barbara Akers, Volunteer, Maui Friends of
the Library Used Book Store

Len Storey (for freeing-up time for Lisa
to edit and design this anthology)

Maui Writers Ink Advisory Committee
(you know who you are)

Made in the USA
Middletown, DE
28 November 2021

52647721R00172